GLORIOUS HEARTS

Hearts first-team pool, pictured at Tynecastle before the Scottish Cup final. (Back row) Ian Jardine, Brian Whittaker, Colin McAdam, Henry Smith, Roddy McDonald, Craig Levein. (Middle row) George Cowie, Andy Watson, Gary Mackay, Walter Kidd, Sandy Clark, Neil Berry, John Robertson, physiotherapist Alan Rae. (Front row) Jimmy Sandison, Billy McKay, Sandy Jardine, manager Alex MacDonald, coach Walter Borthwick, John Colquhoun, Kenny Black.

GLORIOUS HEARTS

The Story of an Incredible Season

Edited by
MIKE AITKEN

Foreword by
TOMMY WALKER, O.B.E.

JOHN DONALD PUBLISHERS LTD
EDINBURGH

ISBN 0 85976 180 0 (Paper)
ISBN 0 85976 181 9 (Cloth)

Acknowledgement: The Editors extend grateful thanks to *The Scotsman* and *The Edinburgh Evening News* for permission to reproduce the illustrations in this book.

Photoset by Quorn Selective Repro, Loughborough. Printed in Great Britain by Bell & Bain Ltd., Glasgow.

Foreword

Although I am not actively involved in football any longer, my affection for Hearts has not diminished and I have derived great satisfaction from the club's efforts in the past season.

There are many, many people like myself in Edinburgh who may not attend matches but who keep in touch with events through newspapers and television.

So it is a considerable honour for me to be associated with this story of a special season in the club's long history — one that could have been the most memorable of all.

I was lucky enough to be manager of Hearts during a period when we collected all the major honours and I appreciate what a boost it is for the city, generally, to have a successful football team.

It was sad that Hearts should lose the Premier Division championship on the last day at Dundee when illness had affected the team so badly, because they deserved to be champions.

I have always held the view that a team can be fortunate to win a cup but the championship is different. Everyone starts on the same mark and a title is won on merit.

Of course, there was disappointment at finishing second but that was a wonderful effort and everyone associated with Hearts ought to be proud of their performances.

I think it is right that Alex MacDonald and Sandy Jardine should be praised for what they have done to re-establish Hearts as a major force. They have done well and I would like to add my congratulations.

Hearts have given us many exciting months in their quest for honours and it seems to me that they are rich enough in young talent to stay in the forefront.

Tommy Walker, O.B.E.

Preface

This book tells the story of a remarkable season in the history of a remarkable club that had lately fallen on unremarkable times. It was conceived in the dark days of winter and put together by the collective effort of sports journalists working in Edinburgh.

The merits or otherwise of 'Glorious Hearts' will be for others to decide, but perhaps it can be claimed here that the work is unique in its appearance so soon after the end of the 1985/86 football season. The authors and the publishers backed a hunch, believing that Hearts' achievements this year would be worthy of record.

Whatever else may be said about the triumphs and the tragedies that came their way, it was unquestionably Hearts' season. The following account is an attempt to describe the personalities, the matches and the background which made hearts beat a little faster throughout the land during that season.

Of course it goes without saying that the authors were honoured when Tommy Walker OBE agreed to write the Foreword. His connection with the club goes back to 1932 when he first signed as a player. He subsequently became assistant manager, manager and a director. He is now retired from football but has a special place in the affections of all those with more than a passing interest in the Hearts.

We hope that this comprehensive account of a momentous year at Tynecastle is simply the first chapter in a new, stirring period for Heart of Midlothian FC.

Mike Aitken, May 1986

Contents

Happy fans gather at the West End of Edinburgh to cheer the team at the end of the most incredible season in the club's history

Glorious Hearts

It was the best of seasons and the worst of eight days in the recent history of Hearts. Having gone 31 games without defeat, enthralled at least half of the city of Edinburgh and gripped much of Scotland with their exploits, the Tynecastle club lost their last two matches to Dundee and Aberdeen and as a result had to settle for second prizes in both the Premier Division championship and the Scottish Cup.

Hearts became possibly the most fêted sporting losers since Henry Cooper lost a title fight to Muhummad Ali. Even in his moment of victory after Aberdeen had emphatically beaten Hearts 3–0 in the Scottish Cup final Alex Ferguson took the trouble to stress: 'No matter what we did out there the season still belongs to Hearts. I'm sick they didn't get anything out of it.'

The 40,000 or so Hearts supporters, who had travelled to Glasgow more in hope than expectation, enjoyed their day out at Hampden and stayed on to cheer their side long after Willie Miller had lifted the Cup for Aberdeen. They knew it was Aberdeen's Cup and Celtic's title, but rightfully felt it was still Hearts' year.

At Dens Park the week before in what was a cruel month of May for the club, Hearts had lost two goals in the last seven minutes of their match against Dundee and let in Celtic to snatch the championship from their grasp on goal difference. The vivid dream of glory which held thousands spellbound for months was abruptly shattered that afternoon.

Grown men broke down and it was, as Ian Wood of *The Scotsman* wittily observed: 'The most tearful audience witnessed at any entertainment, sporting or otherwise, since that moving scene in which ET popped off back to his own little Firhill in the sky.' Having gone 27 championship matches without defeat, Hearts hardly deserved to end up with no tangible reward for their efforts other than a place in the UEFA Cup. However, once the dust has begun to settle on the 1985/86 season, Hearts' achievements won't be forgotten even if the record books don't actually get around to mentioning their name.

Hearts attracted almost 300,000 spectators to watch League football at Tynecastle in the course of a season when they remained unbeaten at home. This was an increase of over 88,000 customers on the previous year. They also took more supporters to away games and became a bigger draw than at any other time in the history of the Premier Division. Hearts' success was good news not only for themselves but also for all the other bank balances of the elite clubs.

Remarkably the disappointment of the last eight days of the season inspired virtually no criticism either from the media or the team's own supporters. In a leading article, *The Scotsman* commented: 'Amid the disappointment, however, the real gains of Hearts' season would not be forgotten. Under the ebullient chairmanship of Wallace Mercer and the young management team of Alex MacDonald and Sandy Jardine, the club has been restored to vigorous health. Where, not so long ago, all was stagnation and lethargy, there is now excitement and life.'

This was a point echoed by David Will, the president of the Scottish Football Association, when he refused to commiserate with Hearts at a dinner to honour Sandy Jardine, the Scottish Football Writers' player of the year. Instead he congratulated the Tynecastle club on 'a magnificent season', one in which their abiding achievement was to bring thousands of spectators back to the game.

Apart from Sandy Jardine's honour, Alex MacDonald was named as the Scottish Brewers' personality manager of the year. Craig Levein was voted by his fellow professionals as the young player of the year and Tommy Walker, the most famous Hearts man of all, was presented with a special merit award for his services to football at the Scottish Players' Union dinner.

In short, it was a year Hearts and their followers would never forget, even if the events at Dens Park on Saturday May 3 were hard to bear.

Something quite remarkable had been set in motion at Tynecastle seven months earlier in the season. Not that drawing with Dundee on October 5 was in itself an extraordinary event, even if Hearts did have a modest record against the Dens Park side. What was significant about that autumn Saturday was that Hearts stopped the rot of back to back defeats from Clydebank and Motherwell and embarked on a record-breaking run of Premier Division games without defeat.

It was clear from Hearts' first game of the season against Saarwellingen in West Germany that Alex MacDonald and Sandy Jardine knew how they wanted to re-shape the side. While injuries and suspensions were to make life hard for the team in August and September — avoiding relegation was a more pertinent issue at that stage than chasing the championship — Hearts appreciated in July that a fresh defensive partnership of Craig Levein and Sandy Jardine could change the way the team played.

The bookmakers, who made Hearts 200-1 outsiders for the title, probably felt that their odds were a shade conservative when the Tynecastle side stuttered through the early weeks of term. Constant changes in most departments of the side brought nothing in the way of continuity; hence why later in the season when the odd injury or suspension cropped up Hearts refused to make two changes when one would do.

The measure of Hearts' achievement can in many ways be best put into a perspective by recalling that the only Scottish bookmaker who compiles a handicap league gave Hearts 26 points of a start over Aberdeen at the start of the season!

The best stories in football are the fairy-tales but the manner in which Hearts came from near bankruptcy to European football possibly would be too far fetched even for the writers of 'Roy Of The Rovers'. For years the plaintive cry: 'What's wrong with Hearts?' echoed noisily round the city of Edinburgh, and for all the talk of sleeping giants there was real concern that the Tynecastle colossus would never waken up.

Thanks to the foresight of the former Hearts chairman Archie Martin, a breakthrough did take place in the spring of 1981. It happened off the field rather than on it and involved the sweeping away of a moribund club structure, to be replaced with a new share issue of 350,000 £1 shares.

This allowed some light to penetrate the gloom of the club's darkest hours in more than a century of football. It was a move which could happily have taken place 20 years earlier, but was better realised late than never. The change in the way Hearts were organised financially opened the door for Wallace Mercer to fight off Kenny Waugh for control and thereafter things would never be the same again at Tynecastle.

Mercer brought an infusion of life and innovation as well as the financial resources which at long last allowed the Hearts football team to be reconstructed along sound lines.

Much credit is paid throughout the course of these pages to the way in which Jardine and MacDonald made shrewd purchases of cast-off players from other clubs and wove them into a brilliant new tapestry.

However, some acknowledgement must also be made to Bobby Moncur's contribution in his time as manager at the beginning of the 1980s. When the club's star was very much in decline, Moncur secured the signings of three young players — John Robertson, Gary Mackay and David Bowman — who went on to have a significant impact on improving Hearts' fortunes.

True, Bowman left to join Coventry before Hearts began seriously to compete for major honours, but the cash from his transfer financed the moves that would lift the Edinburgh club back into contention.

The signings of Craig Levein, John Colquhoun, Sandy Clark, Neil Berry, Brian Whittaker, Ian Jardine and Kenny Black turned Hearts into an outfit who were not only formidably hard to beat but also showed consistent flair in the way they took their chances.

It was a formula which confounded the sceptics — who were still waiting for the bubble to burst two months from the end of the season — and made even Hearts' own followers ask the novel question: 'What's right with Hearts?'

Of course there was no one answer, though many had a stab at defining the Tynecastle club's success. Jim McLean of Dundee United, for instance, was quick to scotch the notion that Hearts' achievements were based simply on effort.

'Give me 11 'ordinary' players such as Hearts have and I don't think they would ever be far from honours', he said. 'It is to their manager's credit that they play to all their strengths. Sandy Clark is a prime example.

'I have always admired his effort, determination and will to win. But Hearts are playing the game to his strengths — which has made him a far better player.'

Playing to the strengths of players who had been found surplus to requirements elsewhere was a vital part of Hearts' game plan. Apart from Clark (who was unrecognisable from the player who had left Ibrox and justified Jim McLean's vote of confidence by playing a towering match in the 3-0 win over United at Tannadice in April) John Colquhoun, Neil Berry and Kenny Black all improved themselves by finding their true positions at Tynecastle.

Alex Ferguson, the Aberdeen and Scotland manager, acknowledged at the turn of the year that whoever won the prizes, there was no doubt that the team of the year was Hearts. He greatly admired the confidence that was instilled amongst Hearts' players in the course of their long unbeaten run and would have happily emulated that quality at international level.

From the professional footballer's angle, Hearts were praised for their tenacity and professionalism. Iain Munro, the captain of Hibs, said: 'In football you have to roll up your sleeves and make your own luck, which, to their credit, is what Hearts have done.'

Richard Gough, tipped as a future Scottish captain by Alex Ferguson and a player with an enormous appetite for the game himself, said: 'Hearts are a team of battlers who work away for each other. And when you get sides of comparable ability meeting, it is the team who show the most heart that usually wins. On top of that, Hearts have been run along thoroughly professional lines.'

Those who argued that Hearts were lucky not to get too many injury problems had a point, but overlooked the situation at the start of the season when all their woes seemed to affect Hearts at once. There were numerous injuries and suspensions when the team slumped to second bottom place in the table; but the longer the unbeaten run went on the fewer players got into trouble with referees and Hearts' disciplinary record improved out of all recognition.

Doubtless this had something to do with not wanting to miss out on the handsome bonus payments that were being earned at Tynecastle. But it is also the case that ill-discipline stems in the main from frustration and disappointment, two moods Hearts didn't have all that much experience of in 1986.

In short, what made Hearts tick was a combination of measured football out of defence and an attacking system that focused on Sandy Clark's strength in winning the ball for either John Robertson or John Colquhoun to supply the finishing touch. As is the case with all good football teams, the Hearts' system was simple, effective and suited the individuals asked to play it.

In addition Hearts had the backing of some of the most enthusiastic supporters in Scotland. They turned many away matches into virtual home games for Hearts and ensured the team always had the kind of atmosphere to bring out the best in them.

Hearts' large following had only been waiting for a sign to turn out in the kind of numbers that had once greeted the halcyon days of the 1950s. Though there was a time when the club had had to tolerate a faction of the support they'd rather have been without, in 1986 the solid citizens of Edinburgh returned to greet the club their grandfathers had warmed to in 1914 when the Hearts' side of the day volunteered to a man for service in the First World War.

Certainly the defeats at Dens Park and Hampden made for a ghoulish end to the season. But the supporters remained in good voice and there was genuine optimism that after a long period in the football wilderness Hearts were at last back to play their part as a force in the game.

A tweak of the nose from Craig Levein for Frank McDougall in the Scottish Cup final at Hampden

The Championship Story — match by match

August 10, 1985

Hearts 1, Celtic 1

Hearts were ill prepared for the first championship match with Walter Kidd, Kenny Black and Roddy McDonald under suspension from the previous season, and a back injury, sustained on the West German tour and to prove extremely serious, cost Malcolm Murray his place.

Despite those problems, Hearts were denied victory by a last-minute goal and the game marked an auspicious debut by winger John Colquhoun against his former club who had sold him for £35,000.

There were no first-match nerves from John as he shot Hearts into a first half lead and went on to outshine every other player on the park.

Sandy Clark missed a chance to put the game beyond Celtic's reach before Hearts suffered a late injury setback. Neil Berry, who had been immense in the middle of the defence, took a knock on the same knee which required an operation in the previous season, and had to quit with six minutes left.

Paul Cherry hardly had time to settle into his defensive role when the match ended with Celtic celebrating a real let-off.

A shot from Paul McStay glanced off a defender to beat Henry Smith, who had dealt so well with the teasing centres from Davie Provan.

Whether Hearts would have won with their original line-up is open to question but Celtic's attack had been contained comfortably with Maurice Johnston easily held.

Even on that opening day, it was evident that Celtic would be hard pressed to maintain a successful challenge.

HEARTS: Smith; Sandison, Whittaker; S. Jardine, Levein, Berry (Cherry); Colquhoun, Watson, Clark, Robertson, Mackay.

CELTIC: Bonner; W. McStay, Burns; Aitken, McAdam, Grant; Provan, P. McStay, Johnston, MacLeod, McClair (McInally).

Referee – H. Alexander, Kilmarnock.

Bookings – S. Jardine, Colquhoun.

7

John Colquhoun shows his delight at scoring against his former team mates. Sandy Clark shares his joy along with Jimmy Sandison and John Robertson

PREMIER LEAGUE

Dundee	2	St. Mirren	1
Motherwell	0	Clydebank	0
Aberdeen	3	Hibernian	0
Hearts	1	Celtic	1
Rangers	1	Dundee United	0

	P	W	D	L	F	A	Pts
Aberdeen	1	1	0	0	3	0	2
Dundee	1	1	0	0	2	1	2
Rangers	1	1	0	0	1	0	2
Clydebank	1	0	1	0	0	0	1
Motherwell	1	0	1	0	0	0	1
Celtic	1	0	1	0	1	1	1
HEARTS	1	0	1	0	1	1	1
Dundee United	1	0	0	1	0	1	0
St. Mirren	1	0	0	1	1	2	0
Hibernian	1	0	0	1	0	3	0

August 17, 1985

St. Mirren 6, Hearts 2

Undoubtedly the worst 90 minutes of the season for Hearts and the biggest defeat under manager Alex MacDonald.

It was a day when the Tynecastle defenders were stricken by some form of palsy in their own penalty area and nothing went right.

There was no quick bath for the players at the finish. They were given a severe telling off by the manager who took fully 40 minutes to unlock the dressing-room door.

More than four years had passed since Hearts were hit for six by Celtic at Parkhead and it was a result which shook the team badly.

Roddy McDonald for the injured Berry was the only change yet they played sloppily and gifted several goals to Saints.

In the early minutes, John Robertson swept through with only goalkeeper Campbell Money to beat and his miss was an omen for the entire game.

What made it worse was the fact that Hearts actually scored first in 14 minutes when John Colquhoun thrashed home a pass from John Robertson.

But errors in defence allowed Speirs and Godfrey to score with headers and a fine run by Gallacher enabled McGarvey to make it 3-1 by half time.

There was no way back for Hearts once Fitzpatrick slipped in a McGarvey pass seven minutes into the second half. The floodgates were open as Clarke and Rooney took the total to six with 18 minutes left. Thankfully, the remaining goal was for Hearts with Robertson on target.

HEARTS: Smith; Sandison, Whittaker; S. Jardine, R. McDonald, Levein; Colquhoun, Watson, Clark, Robertson, Mackay.

ST. MIRREN: Money; Wilson, Hamilton; Rooney, Godfrey, Clarke; Fitzpatrick, Mackie, McGarvey, Gallacher, Speirs.

Referee – A. Ferguson, Giffnock.

PREMIER LEAGUE

Celtic	2	Motherwell	1
Clydebank	4	Dundee	0
Dundee United	1	Aberdeen	1
Hibernian	1	Rangers	3
St. Mirren	6	Hearts	2

	P	W	D	L	F	A	Pts
Rangers	2	2	0	0	4	1	4
Clydebank	2	1	1	0	4	0	3
Aberdeen	2	1	1	0	4	1	3
Celtic	2	1	1	0	3	2	3
St. Mirren	2	1	0	1	7	4	2
Dundee	2	1	0	1	2	5	2
Dundee United	2	0	1	1	1	2	1
Motherwell	2	0	1	1	1	2	1
HEARTS	2	0	1	1	3	7	1
Hibernian	2	0	0	2	1	6	0

August 24, 1985

Rangers 3, Hearts 1

Rangers kept their perfect League record in one of the most controversial games of the season. Five bookings had been handed out before a second half flare-up resulted in Walter Kidd, Sandy Clark and Ally McCoist being sent off.

Although fists flew in an unwanted incident, Hearts were annoyed that Clark should be shown the red card and even angrier when the centre forward received a three-match ban with skipper Kidd after all three offenders had been called to a special SFA probe.

This suspension came on top of the automatic one-match suspension so it was a costly afternoon for the club. Oddly enough, the SFA did not intervene at any other stage of the season though there were matches worthy of investigation for rough play.

George Cowie took over in midfield from Gary Mackay and his enthusiastic style ensured that Rangers had no long-term control in that area. Indeed, Hearts were in front again from a John Robertson free kick just before half time. He was pulled down by McPherson on the edge of the box; the home defender was booked and Robbo fired the deflected shot past Walker.

The substitution of the rugged McKinnon for Durrant on the hour swung the contest in Rangers' favour. Within five minutes, full back Burns stormed through on a solo run to equalise.

Williamson added a second in 69 minutes and Hearts were up against it when, suddenly, they were reduced to nine men.

Hearts had Paul Cherry on in place of Brian Whittaker and John Colquhoun gave way to Brian McNaughton but the only other goal came from Williamson. Manager MacDonald was pleased with the team's determination if not the result.

RANGERS: Walker; Burns, Munro; McPherson, Paterson, Bell; McCoist, Russell, Williamson, Durrant (McKinnon), Cooper.

HEARTS: Smith; Kidd, Whittaker (Cherry); S. Jardine, R. McDonald, Levein; Colquhoun (McNaughton), Watson, Clark, Cowie, Robertson.

Referee – D. D. Hope, Erskine.

Sent off – Kidd, Clark. Bookings – Kidd, Clark, Watson, Robertson.

PREMIER LEAGUE

Aberdeen	1	Motherwell	1
Clydebank	0	Celtic	2
Dundee United	2	Dundee	0
Hibernian	2	St. Mirren	3
Rangers	3	Hearts	1

	P	W	D	L	F	A	Pts
Rangers	3	3	0	0	7	2	6
Celtic	3	2	1	0	5	2	5
St. Mirren	3	2	0	1	10	6	4
Aberdeen	3	1	2	0	5	2	4
Clydebank	3	1	1	1	4	2	3
Dundee United	3	1	1	1	3	2	3
Motherwell	3	0	2	1	2	3	2
Dundee	3	1	0	2	2	7	2
HEARTS	3	0	1	2	4	10	1
Hibernian	3	0	0	3	3	9	0

August 31, 1985

Hearts 2, Hibernian 1

An overdue first win for Hearts who were able to celebrate the continuation of their derby day domination through a late goal by the alert Sandy Clark.

He had missed the midweek Skol tie with Stirling Albion and Hearts were glad that the bustling Clark was available to score in his third successive match against Hibs.

It was a slip by substitute Rae on the muddy surface that allowed Clark to grab the all-important goal and keep Hibs pointless at the foot of the table.

The Easter Road men lost Kane in only five minutes with a depressed jaw fracture in a clash with George Cowie, while Craig Levein played despite a bout of flu during the week.

It was a typical derby struggle in which Hearts had the vital upper hand in midfield. Yet again, the team struck first and John Colquhoun confirmed his favouritism with the fans by scoring his third goal in four championship matches.

Durie equalised for Hibs, having dropped back to fill Kane's place though he resumed his role as an orthodox striker in the second half.

The pace of Colquhoun and John Robertson consistently troubled an uncertain Hibs defence and Gary Mackay contributed in his usual subtle fashion as a replacement for Andy Watson.

It was a modest yet sportingly contested game and top referee Brian McGinlay made sure he was always in total control. Only George Cowie was cautioned which confirmed the referee's strong hand.

HEARTS: Smith; Kidd, Cowie; S. Jardine, R. McDonald, Levein; Colquhoun, Watson (Mackay), Clark, Robertson, Black.

HIBS: Rough; Sneddon, Munro; Kane (Rae), Fulton, Hunter; Weir, Brazil, Cowan, Durie, Harris.

Referee – B. R. McGinlay, Balfron.

Booking – Cowie.

PREMIER LEAGUE

Celtic	1	Rangers	1
Dundee	1	Aberdeen	3
Hearts	2	Hibernian	1
Motherwell	0	Dundee United	1
St. Mirren	0	Clydebank	2

	P	W	D	L	F	A	Pts
Rangers	4	3	1	0	8	3	7
Aberdeen	4	2	2	0	8	3	6
Celtic	4	2	2	0	6	3	6
Clydebank	4	2	1	1	6	2	5
Dundee United	4	2	1	1	4	2	5
St. Mirren	4	2	0	2	10	8	4
HEARTS	4	1	1	2	6	11	3
Motherwell	4	0	2	2	2	4	2
Dundee	4	1	0	3	3	10	2
Hibernian	4	0	0	4	4	11	0

September 7, 1985

Aberdeen 3, Hearts 0

Champions Aberdeen were flattered by the margin of their victory as manager Alex Ferguson readily admitted after the game in which the odds were piled high against Hearts.

They had to contend with the ban on Walter Kidd and Sandy Clark, an injury to John Robertson and a loss of form by Gary Mackay, plus the fact that the club was denied space for the fans through construction work at one end.

Nevertheless, Hearts overcame a sticky start to put tremendous pressure on the renowned Aberdeen defence. Brian McNaughton had a couple of chances and Leighton was the busier goalkeeper.

So it was rather bad luck that the Dons should break the deadlock in 32 minutes with a headed goal from Stark.

McNaughton had a luckless day, missing another chance after the referee refused him a confident penalty claim when Miller pulled him down. Paul Cherry, too, shot wide with Leighton to beat.

Hearts had cause to regret their poor finishing once Wright replaced Stark for the newcomer had scarcely warmed up when he put Aberdeen two up with 16 minutes left.

Gary Mackay's introduction had no effect on the result though Black headed a late third goal.

Kenny Black was carried off in the final minutes with a leg injury having clashed with Cooper.

ABERDEEN: Leighton; McKimmie, Mitchell; Stark (Wright), McLeish, Miller; Black, Simpson, McDougall, Bett, Hewitt.

HEARTS: Smith; Cowie, Whittaker; S. Jardine, R. McDonald, Levein; Colquhoun (Mackay), Watson, McNaughton, Cherry, Black (Sandison).

Referee – M. Delaney, Cleland.

Bookings – McDonald, Levein, Black.

PREMIER LEAGUE

Aberdeen	3	Hearts	0
Dundee United	2	Clydebank	1
Hibernian	0	Celtic	5
Motherwell	1	Dundee	3
Rangers	3	St. Mirren	0

	P	W	D	L	F	A	Pts
Rangers	5	4	1	0	11	3	9
Aberdeen	5	3	2	0	11	3	8
Celtic	5	3	2	0	11	3	8
Dundee United	5	3	1	1	6	3	7
Clydebank	5	2	1	2	7	4	5
St. Mirren	5	2	0	3	10	11	4
Dundee	5	2	0	3	6	11	4
HEARTS	5	1	1	3	6	14	3
Motherwell	5	0	2	3	3	7	2
Hibernian	5	0	0	5	4	16	0

September 14, 1985

Hearts 2, Dundee United 0

There was a minute's silence before the game in memory of Jock Stein, the Scotland manager who had died immediately after the World Cup tie with Wales at Cardiff on the previous Wednesday.

The fans paid a most sincere tribute before Hearts gave the first clear indication that there would be little joy for visitors to Tynecastle and went on to win handsomely with a patched up team.

Kenny Black was unfit, George Cowie came off the treatment table to play and John Robertson could not be risked for the full 90 minutes.

However, there was the bonus of a return by Neil Berry, who had been sidelined for five weeks – and sorely missed.

As United had taken six points off Hearts in the previous season, they were entitled to approach the game with a good deal of confidence. It proved to be misplaced.

Hearts had decided that it was essential to capture home points and reinforced this aim once Roddy McDonald steered a long header past McAlpine inside two minutes from a corner by John Colquhoun.

United's short-passing was accurate though ineffective and Hearts always had the greater desire to win. They found a lot of space down the right as Colquhoun dragged his marker into the middle of the field.

Ten minutes after half time, Hearts used Robertson for Brian McNaughton in the belief that his thigh complaint would stand the strain. It worked because Robbo lobbed in the crucial second goal 11 minutes from time after another Colquhoun corner.

Berry's industry in midfield and the defensive work of Henry Smith and Sandy Jardine kept Hearts in command and the overall determination was tremendous.

HEARTS: Smith; Cowie, Whittaker; S. Jardine, R. McDonald, Levein; Colquhoun, Watson, McNaughton (Robertson), Berry, Cherry.

DUNDEE UNITED: McAlpine; Malpas, Kirkwood; Gough, Hegarty, Narey; Bannon, Milne (Clark), Redford (Beedie), Sturrock, Dodds.

Referee – J. R. Renton, Cowdenbeath.

Booking – R. McDonald.

Brian Whittaker outjumps everyone to pressure Dundee United's defence with Roddy McDonald by his side

PREMIER LEAGUE

Celtic	2	Aberdeen	1
Clydebank	0	Rangers	1
Dundee	1	Hibernian	0
Hearts	2	Dundee United	0
St. Mirren	4	Motherwell	1

	P	W	D	L	F	A	Pts
Rangers	6	5	1	0	12	3	11
Celtic	6	4	2	0	12	4	10
Aberdeen	6	3	2	1	13	5	8
Dundee United	6	3	1	2	6	5	7
St. Mirren	6	3	0	3	14	12	6
Dundee	6	3	0	3	7	11	6
Clydebank	6	2	1	3	7	5	5
HEARTS	6	2	1	3	8	14	5
Motherwell	6	0	2	4	4	11	2
Hibernian	6	0	0	6	4	17	0

A relaxed moment during pre-season training

September 21, 1985

Motherwell 2, Hearts 1

Monsoon weather throughout Scotland caused some matches to be postponed but play was possible on a very wet Fir Park.

Motherwell were without a win and it looked an ideal opportunity for Hearts to pick up their first away points.

Still without their suspended pair, Hearts were matched by vigorous opponents, and an injury to Roddy McDonald just before half time was no help. Little did the big centre half realise that his leg knock would cost him his place until February!

Roddy's misfortune meant a debut chance for Ian Jardine and a reshuffle in the Tynecastle defence. The interval produced another shock in the shape of a bomb scare which necessitated a police search of the covered enclosure.

A 20-minute half-time break seemed to have done no harm to Hearts who moved briskly into the lead in 48 minutes. And it was newcomer Jardine who pounced on an error by McCart to celebrate his promotion.

Sadly, it was a short-term lead. Within a minute, Harrow equalised after the Hearts defence had become muddled in trying to clear a corner kick.

That was rich encouragement for Motherwell who scored quickly through Gahagan with a 12 yards shot. Although Hearts had half an hour left to gather themselves, they had lost the midfield struggle and offered too little help to John Robertson.

Brian McNaughton replaced Andy Watson for a final assault but Motherwell held on grimly to their advantage.

MOTHERWELL: Gardiner; Dornan, Wishart; Doyle, Forbes, McCart; Gahagan, Reilly, Harrow, Wright, Blair.

HEARTS: Smith; Cowie, Whittaker; S. Jardine, R. McDonald (I. Jardine), Levein; Watson (McNaughton), Robertson, Colquhoun, Berry, Cherry.

Referee – R. B. Valentine, Dundee.

Bookings – Cowie, Cherry.

PREMIER LEAGUE

Aberdeen	1	St. Mirren	1
Motherwell	2	Hearts	1
Rangers	0	Dundee	1

	P	W	D	L	F	A	Pts
Rangers	7	5	1	1	12	4	11
Celtic	6	4	2	0	13	4	10
Aberdeen	7	3	3	1	13	6	9
Dundee	7	4	0	3	8	11	8
St. Mirren	7	3	1	3	15	13	7
Dundee United	6	3	1	2	6	5	7
Clydebank	6	2	1	3	7	5	5
HEARTS	7	2	1	4	9	16	5
Motherwell	7	1	2	4	6	12	4
Hibernian	6	0	0	6	4	17	0

Pre-season training on the sand dunes. Sandy Jardine keeps an eye out for slackers!

September 28, 1985

Clydebank 1, Hearts 0

Manager Alex MacDonald had made it clear that he intended to stick to odd appearances in the reserve team and that it would take an emergency situation to choose himself for League duty.

He found himself in a predicament at Kilbowie, for the return of Sandy Clark, Walter Kidd and Kenny Black was offset by the injuries to George Cowie, Roddy McDonald and Ian Jardine.

Alex sat on the bench for most of the time but took over from John Colquhoun late on in his one brief outing.

Sadly, his influence couldn't save Hearts from another defeat that ought to have been avoided. They dominated most of the game only to concede a last-minute goal to substitute Lloyd.

There was no time to salvage even a point but what angered Hearts was the refusal of a cast-iron penalty when Sandy Clark was fouled. Even the

Clydebank players were astonished to see the referee ignore the incident.

Both teams had the ball in the net in the first half shortly after Clydebank's McCabe was forced to quit through injury.

But the efforts by Conroy and Clark were wiped out for previous infringements. A slack passback by Black nearly gifted a goal to Clydebank in the early minutes of the second half and only the alertness of Henry Smith saved the day.

Neil Berry worked ceaselessly in midfield to find a gap in the home defence but a draw looked guaranteed when Lloyd struck.

Significantly, Sandy Jardine predicted that results must improve with the players showing such determination and dedication. The words of a true prophet!

CLYDEBANK: Gallacher; Dickson (Lloyd), Given; Fallon, Treanor, Maher; Ronald, Shanks, Larnach, Conroy, McCabe (Hughes).

HEARTS: Smith; Kidd, Whittaker; S. Jardine, Berry, Levein; Colquhoun (A. MacDonald), Watson, Clark, Robertson, Black.

Referee – T. Muirhead, Stenhousemuir.

PREMIER LEAGUE

Clydebank	1	Hearts	0
Dundee	0	Celtic	2
Hibernian	1	Motherwell	0
Rangers	0	Aberdeen	3
St. Mirren	1	Dundee United	0

	P	W	D	L	F	A	Pts
Celtic	7	5	2	0	15	4	12
Aberdeen	8	4	3	1	16	6	11
Rangers	8	5	1	2	12	7	11
St. Mirren	8	4	1	3	16	13	9
Dundee	8	4	0	4	8	13	8
Clydebank	7	3	1	3	8	5	7
Dundee United	7	3	1	3	6	6	7
HEARTS	8	2	1	5	9	17	5
Motherwell	8	1	2	5	6	13	4
Hibernian	7	1	0	6	5	17	2

October 5, 1985

Hearts 1, Dundee 1

Gary Mackay and Ian Jardine returned for Hearts on the day that marked John Robertson's 100th League appearance. It was also his 150th first team match with his goal record standing at 69.

But there was no celebration for Robbo as Hearts battled grimly to try and master their jinx team. Heads drooped slightly when a defensive error allowed Dundee to take a swift lead in 11 minutes.

Henry Smith had made an excellent save from Shannon before Rafferty exploited a lot of right-wing room and his cross led to McWilliams shooting into the net from 12 yards.

Hearts knew it would be an uphill struggle and were relieved that Smith reached a net-bound header from Harvey.

Suddenly, it was all tense and tough and four players were booked in the space of seven minutes. Brian Whittaker was the only Hearts offender and McWilliams had a bad tackle on John Colquhoun, who required attention for the second time in the first half.

Hearts were guilty of making too many mistakes and the fans were unhappy with the trend of the play.

Still, the gloom disappeared in 55 minutes as Ian Jardine delivered one of his valuable goals with a header which left Geddes helpless.

Mackay urged his teammates towards a winner with his clever passes and good ballwork but Hearts had to be content with a draw.

Hearts had completed the first round of fixtures with only six points and 10 goals to occupy third bottom place and no fewer than 19 players had been involved, such was the crop of injuries.

HEARTS: Smith; Kidd, Whittaker; S. Jardine, Berry, Levein; Colquhoun, I. Jardine, Clark, Mackay, Robertson.

DUNDEE: Geddes; Shannon (Forsyth), Glennie; McCormack, Smith, Duffy; Rafferty, Hendrie, Harvey, Connor, McWilliams.

Referee – A. Ferguson, Giffnock.

Booking – Whittaker.

Dundee seem determined to stop John Robertson in this incident with Jim Duffy leading the charge

PREMIER LEAGUE

Aberdeen	3	Clydebank	1
Celtic	2	St. Mirren	0
Dundee United	2	Hibernian	2
Hearts	1	Dundee	1
Motherwell	0	Rangers	3

	P	W	D	L	F	A	Pts
Celtic	8	6	2	0	17	4	14
Aberdeen	9	5	3	1	19	7	13
Rangers	9	6	1	2	15	7	13
St. Mirren	9	4	1	4	16	15	9
Dundee	9	4	1	4	9	14	9
Dundee United	8	3	2	3	8	8	8
Clydebank	9	3	1	5	9	13	7
HEARTS	9	2	2	5	10	18	6
Hibernian	9	2	1	6	12	19	5
Motherwell	9	1	2	6	6	16	4

Oct. 1 — Hibernian 5, Clydebank 0

October 12, 1985

Celtic 0, Hearts 1

A day of both triumph and worry at Parkhead! Celtic surrendered their unbeaten record as Hearts won away in the championship for the first time this season – and broke their winning duck in Premier League matches at the ground.

But the worry stemmed from a second-half injury sustained by matchwinner John Robertson who damaged his neck in a duel with Roy Aitken.

It looked extremely serious and Hearts physiotherapist Alan Rae was so concerned that he didn't wait for permission from referee Duncan to dash to the player's aid.

Robbo was carried off on a stretcher and taken immediately to hospital by ambulance for tests. Happily, the diagnosis was severe bruising which was a huge relief to all concerned.

John was able to listen to a commentary on the match en route to hospital and knew that his colleagues were hanging on to the points. He was hurt with 20 minutes to go and Andy Watson took over in what became a testing period.

A considerable period of injury time was allowed for the stoppage and both Henry Smith and Kenny Black were booked for time-wasting in the tense finish.

Smith had superb saves from McGugan and Johnston though, generally, the shooting of the Celtic side gave little cause for anxiety.

Hearts defended sensibly and worked with customary zeal to protect the first-half goal which came from their one chance to that point.

John Colquhoun and Sandy Clark provided the build-up after 33 minutes and sure-shot Robbo whipped the ball past Bonner from eight yards.

It was a vital result which indicated that Hearts were capable of winning anywhere with a settled team.

CELTIC: Bonner; McGrain, Burns; Aitken, McGugan, Grant; Provan, McStay, Johnston, MacLeod, McClair.

HEARTS: Smith; Kidd, Whittaker; S. Jardine, Berry, Levein; Colquhoun (Black), I. Jardine, Clark, Mackay, Robertson (Watson).

Referee – J. Duncan, Gorebridge.

Bookings – Berry, S. Jardine, Smith, Black.

B

Celtic's Mo Johnston hasn't a look-in as Craig Levein soars to head the ball to safety

PREMIER LEAGUE

Celtic	0	Hearts	1
Clydebank	1	Motherwell	1
Dundee United	1	Rangers	1
Hibernian	1	Aberdeen	1
St. Mirren	1	Dundee	0

	P	W	D	L	F	A	Pts
Aberdeen	10	5	4	1	20	8	14
Celtic	9	6	2	1	17	5	14
Rangers	10	6	2	2	16	8	14
St. Mirren	10	5	1	4	17	15	11
Dundee United	9	3	3	3	9	9	9
Dundee	10	4	1	5	9	15	9
Clydebank	10	3	2	5	10	14	8
HEARTS	10	3	2	5	11	18	8
Hibernian	10	2	2	6	13	20	6
Motherwell	10	1	3	6	7	17	5

October 19, 1985

Hearts 3, St. Mirren 0

Not only did John Robertson make an amazing recovery from his neck injury but he destroyed St. Mirren with two goals early in the second half to take his personal score in League football to 50.

It was his first double since the UEFA Cup tie against Paris St. Germain a year earlier and Robbo nearly made it a hat trick when a shot in the closing minutes came off the woodwork.

Three St. Mirren players and Craig Levein were booked in a hard, rugged first half and it was in the second period that Hearts really turned on the style.

Such sweet revenge for the six-goal hammering at Paisley and it began two minutes after half time. Ian Jardine and Sandy Clark combined for Robbo to lob the ball behind Money from inside the penalty area.

That was all the encouragement Hearts wanted and goal number two followed in 53 minutes. Clark nodded a cross from Brian Whittaker into Robertson's path and a vicious hook shot flew into the net from 12 yards.

A high-kicking exhibition from Gary Mackay against St. Mirren

Henry Smith, who had made one excellent save from Gallacher, hurt his back in a clash with Godfrey and both players required attention.

Hearts were in cavalier mood with the points clearly won and Saints knew their task was a hopeless one.

Gary Mackay, spraying his deft passes left and right, completed a most polished display with a lovely third goal – his first of the season.

Hearts moved up two places into sixth spot and were in earnest pursuit of the clubs above them.

HEARTS: Smith; Kidd, Whittaker; S. Jardine, Berry, Levein; Colquhoun, I. Jardine, Clark, Mackay, Robertson.

ST. MIRREN: Money; Cooper, Hamilton; Rooney (Abercromby), Godfrey, Clarke; Fitzpatrick, McDowall, McGarvey, Gallacher, Spiers (Mackie).

Referee – J. R. Renton, Cowdenbeath.

Booking – Levein.

PREMIER LEAGUE

Aberdeen	3	Dundee United	2
Dundee	2	Clydebank	0
Hearts	3	St. Mirren	0
Motherwell	1	Celtic	2
Rangers	1	Hibernian	2

	P	W	D	L	F	A	Pts
Aberdeen	11	6	4	1	23	10	16
Celtic	10	7	2	1	19	6	16
Rangers	11	6	2	3	17	10	14
St. Mirren	11	5	1	5	17	18	11
Dundee	11	5	1	5	11	15	11
HEARTS	11	4	2	5	14	18	10
Dundee United	10	3	3	4	11	12	9
Clydebank	11	3	2	6	10	16	8
Hibernian	11	3	2	6	15	21	8
Motherwell	11	1	3	7	8	19	5

October 30, 1985

Hearts 1, Aberdeen 0

Aberdeen had beaten Hibs in the Skol League Cup final at Hampden on the Sunday and arrived at Tynecastle in buoyant mood in the role of League leaders.

But they were not so happy at the finish after losing to Hearts in a championship game for the first time since 1978.

Hearts' managerial team of Alex MacDonald and Sandy Jardine had seen the Dons win nine and draw three of the 12 matches since they took over and it was lucky 13 for them.

It was only Aberdeen's second loss in 20 matches this season and, at the time, nobody realised the significance of the result.

Hearts were to build on this all-action display and Aberdeen had no complaints about the result, for they never equalled the home team's thirst for victory. Sandy Clark refused to give Willie Miller and Alex McLeish any peace and the international pair were unsettled by his restless roving.

Hearts, on the other hand, were magnificent at the back and Sandy

Up goes Craig Levein to outjump Jim Leighton for the only goal of the game against Aberdeen

Jardine was prompted to push the international claims of Craig Levein for his outstanding play.

Fittingly, perhaps, it was the big Fifer who produced the matchwinning goal in only 14 minutes. He rose for a corner by John Colquhoun and beat Jim Leighton in the jump to the joy of his colleagues and customers.

It was a tough game, not especially well refereed, and five names went into the book.

Aberdeen became frustrated as Hearts buttoned up the points and the only scare came in injury time when Henry Smith saved brilliantly from Simpson.

Despite the poor start to the season, Hearts were within four points of the table top thanks to a settled team.

HEARTS: Smith; Kidd, Whittaker; S. Jardine, Berry, Levein; Colquhoun, I. Jardine (Black), Clark, Robertson, Mackay.

ABERDEEN: Leighton; McKimmie, Angus (Bett); Gray, McLeish, Miller; Weir, Simpson, McDougall (Wright), Cooper, Hewitt.

Referee – L. Thow, Ayr.

Bookings – Whittaker, Black.

John Robertson and Sandy Clark shake up the Aberdeen defence at Tynecastle

PREMIER LEAGUE

Celtic	0	Dundee United	3
Dundee	3	Motherwell	1
St. Mirren	2	Rangers	1

Played Oct. 26

Oct. 30

Hearts	1	Aberdeen	0
Clydebank	2	Hibernian	4

	P	W	D	L	F	A	Pts
Aberdeen	12	6	4	2	23	11	16
Celtic	11	7	2	2	19	9	16
Rangers	12	6	2	4	18	12	14
St. Mirren	12	6	1	5	19	19	13
Dundee	12	6	1	5	14	16	13
HEARTS	12	5	2	5	15	18	12
Dundee United	11	4	3	4	14	12	11
Hibernian	12	4	2	6	19	23	10
Clydebank	12	3	2	7	12	20	8
Motherwell	12	1	3	8	9	22	5

November 2, 1985

Dundee United 1, Hearts 1

Hearts were unchanged for the fifth game in succession which was a far cry from the patchwork days at the start of the season. And the settled, more confident team almost repeated their Parkhead success.

They led until the last minute of the match when Scotland defender Richard Gough salvaged a point for United.

Nevertheless, it was a first-class result and further proof that Hearts were heading for the top half of the table in a hurry.

Hearts had a couple of anxious moments in the first half. Henry Smith saved from Sturrock who had looked offside and Milne crashed the ball against the post after a superb solo effort.

However, John Robertson and Kenny Black troubled Thomson in the United goal just before half time. The substitution of Beedle for Redford signalled that all was not well in the home camp and they were more distressed once Hearts scored in 67 minutes.

John Colquhoun, Gary Mackay and Neil Berry were all in the thick of hectic pressure until the ball broke to Ian Jardine whose 20 yarder flashed into the net.

It was his third goal in only six League outings and, already, his cannonball shooting from outwith the penalty box had become a huge asset.

John Robertson was replaced by Kenny Black and United were mighty relieved to achieve a great escape with their last-gasp goal.

DUNDEE UNITED: Thomson; Malpas, Holt; Gough, Hegarty, Narey; Bannon, Milne, Dodds, Sturrock, Redford (Beedie).

HEARTS: Smith; Kidd, Whittaker; S. Jardine, Berry, Levein; Colquhoun, I. Jardine, Clark, Mackay, Robertson (Black).

Referee – R. B. Valentine, Dundee.

PREMIER LEAGUE

Aberdeen	4	Celtic	1
Dundee United	1	Hearts	1
Hibernian	2	Dundee	1
Motherwell	3	St. Mirren	1
Rangers	0	Clydebank	0

	P	W	D	L	F	A	Pts
Aberdeen	13	7	4	2	27	12	18
Celtic	12	7	2	3	20	13	16
Rangers	13	6	3	4	18	12	15
St. Mirren	13	6	1	6	20	22	13
HEARTS	13	5	3	5	16	19	13
Dundee	13	6	1	6	15	18	13
Dundee United	12	4	4	4	15	13	12
Hibernian	13	5	2	6	21	24	12
Clydebank	13	3	3	7	12	20	9
Motherwell	13	2	3	8	12	23	7

November 9, 1985

Hibernian 0, Hearts 0

There might have been disappointment that Hearts failed to score a goal but this, after all, was a local derby and both sides seemed quite satisfied with the result.

However, there was one great chance created in the game and Sandy Clark missed it with 16 minutes to play.

In fairness, the pitch had been made slippy by heavy rain so conditions were tricky. Still, Gary Mackay and John Robertson carved up the Easter Road defence to leave goalkeeper Rough stranded. All Sandy had to do was slide the ball into the net ... but it trailed just wide.

Nevertheless, it was an away point gained and Hibs hadn't won against the MacDonald-Jardine management team.

Robbo was fit following an injury scare at Tannadice and Hibs recalled Rae who had been banned for the three previous games.

Like most derby clashes, it was hard and competitive without being very skilful. Determination played an important part and Hibs were anxious to

Spot the face behind the ball. It's Henry Smith all right with Craig Levein and Walter Kidd on hand against Hibs

protect their winning run which had yielded 12 points from a possible 14.

As was written at the time, this was a duel between the two in-form teams in the country. Rough had a smart save from John Colquhoun a few minutes from the break and Cowan had a reasonable opportunity for Hibs.

Both teams introduced a substitute in the hope of ending the deadlock, but they were so well matched that even the six bookings worked out even.

It was a day when experience counted with Sandy Jardine and Iain Munro the most accomplished performers on the field.

HIBERNIAN: Rough; Sneddon, Munro; Rae, Fulton, Hunter; Kane, Chisholm, Cowan, Durie, McBride (Brazil).

HEARTS: Smith; Kidd, Whittaker; S. Jardine, Berry, Levein; Colquhoun (Black), I. Jardine, Clark, Mackay, Robertson.

Referee – G. B. Smith, Edinburgh.

Bookings – Whittaker, Levein, I. Jardine.

PREMIER LEAGUE

Aberdeen	4	Dundee	1
Dundee United	3	Motherwell	0
Hibernian	0	Hearts	0
Rangers	3	Celtic	0

	P	W	D	L	F	A	Pts
Aberdeen	14	8	4	2	31	13	20
Rangers	14	7	3	4	21	12	17
Celtic	13	7	2	4	20	16	16
Dundee United	13	5	4	4	18	13	14
HEARTS	14	5	4	5	16	19	14
St. Mirren	13	6	1	6	20	22	13
Hibernian	14	5	3	6	21	24	13
Dundee	14	6	1	7	16	22	13
Clydebank	13	3	3	7	12	20	9
Motherwell	14	2	3	9	12	26	7

November 16, 1985

Hearts 3, Rangers 0

This would have been a most special day even if Hearts had not walloped Rangers by a three-goal margin.

For it marked the 1000th senior appearance of assistant manager Sandy Jardine – the first Scottish player to reach that amazing milestone.

Most of these matches had been played in Rangers colours which meant the entire audience of more than 23,000 appreciated his feat. There was a huge ovation for Sandy and a pre-match presentation of crystal, one of many gifts to acclaim his great day.

The script for the game matched the occasion with Sandy on the winning side. Hearts were much superior and should have won by a wider margin. John Robertson, usually such a deadly finisher, missed two good early chances on the greasy pitch but it was only a first-half reprieve for Rangers.

After 13 minutes of the second period, McPherson and Walker became muddled in trying to clear a throw from Ian Jardine and Sandy Clark whipped a 10 yards lob into the net.

McMinn replaced Williamson in the Ibrox attack but nothing could stop the rampant Hearts. Clark scored a brilliant second goal in 79 minutes when he pulled down a cross from John Colquhoun before smashing the ball past Walker.

With Sandy Jardine and Brian Whittaker in outstanding mood, the home goal was hardly ever threatened and Hearts fans were in their element.

A minute from time, John Robertson made them happier with a third goal which squared up the goals account for the first time since August. And there were plenty more goals to come in the weeks and months ahead.

HEARTS: Smith; Kidd, Whittaker; S. Jardine, Berry, Levein; Colquhoun, I. Jardine, Clark, Mackay, Robertson.

RANGERS: Walker; Dawson, Munro; McPherson, McKinnon, Bell; McCoist, Russell, Williamson (McMinn), Durrant, Cooper.

Referee – T. Muirhead, Stenhousemuir.

Booking – Whittaker.

PREMIER LEAGUE

Celtic	2	Clydebank	0
Dundee	0	Dundee United	3
Hearts	3	Rangers	0
Motherwell	1	Aberdeen	1
St. Mirren	1	Hibernian	3

Nov. 13

Clydebank	1	St. Mirren	1

	P	W	D	L	F	A	Pts
Aberdeen	15	8	5	2	32	14	21
Celtic	14	8	2	4	22	16	18
Rangers	15	7	3	5	21	15	17
Dundee United	14	6	4	4	21	13	16
HEARTS	15	6	4	5	19	19	16
Hibernian	15	6	3	6	24	25	15
Dundee	15	6	1	8	16	25	13
Clydebank	15	3	4	8	13	23	10
Motherwell	15	2	4	9	13	27	8

November 23, 1985

Hearts 3, Motherwell 0

If Motherwell, who were anchored at the foot of the table, had any chance of cracking Hearts' unbeaten home record, it disappeared before half time with the dismissal of Raymond Blair.

The Fir Park forward was booked for the second time as the interval approached and Motherwell, already trailing by a goal, knew they were beaten.

Hearts were forced to alter the team which had taken 11 points from seven games because left back Brian Whittaker was suspended for three matches.

But Kenny Black, who had appeared as a substitute four times in that run, simply slotted into the vacancy to keep up the excellent work.

Hearts took 33 minutes to outwit a packed defence and it was Sandy Clark who headed the goal from a cross by Sandy Jardine.

The pressure was incessant yet Motherwell held out until 56 minutes. Neil Barry had a go from John Colquhoun's cross and the ball rebounded kindly for Clark to clip in number two.

A typical Ian Jardine shot from a pass by Gary Mackay made the scoreline more impressive after 63 minutes and Henry Smith completed his sixth shut-out in seven League matches.

At the same time, Hearts were climbing the table fast and this victory hoisted them into fourth place.

Early leaders Rangers were pushed into fifth place and it was gratifying to collect no cautions after picking up 11 yellow cards in seven outings.

HEARTS: Smith; Kidd, Black; S. Jardine, Berry, Levein; Colquhoun, I. Jardine, Clark, Mackay, Robertson.

MOTHERWELL: Gardiner; Wishart, Murray (Kennedy); Dornan, Forbes, McCart; Gahagan, MacLeod, Harrow, Wright, Blair.

Referee – H. Williamson, Renfrew.

A 50-50 ball between Sandy Clark and Motherwell centre-half, Graeme Forbes

PREMIER LEAGUE

Celtic	1	Hibernian	1
Clydebank	1	Dundee United	2
Dundee	3	Rangers	2
Hearts	3	Motherwell	0
St. Mirren	1	Aberdeen	0

	P	W	D	L	F	A	Pts
Aberdeen	16	8	5	3	32	15	21
Celtic	15	8	3	4	23	17	19
Dundee United	15	7	4	4	23	14	18
HEARTS	16	7	4	5	22	19	18
Rangers	16	7	3	6	23	18	17
Hibernian	16	6	4	6	25	26	16
St. Mirren	16	7	2	7	23	26	16
Dundee	16	7	1	8	19	27	15
Clydebank	16	3	4	9	14	25	10
Motherwell	16	2	4	10	13	30	8

November 30, 1985

Hearts 4, Clydebank 1

A light covering of snow had disappeared to leave the pitch in a treacherous condition. Players found difficulty in staying upright when the ball wasn't near them.

So it was a lottery, especially in the first 20 minutes, though heavy rain helped to make the conditions easier.

Hearts were prepared to take risks whatever the state of the surface and the points were wrapped up by half time as they tackled the opposition in a businesslike manner.

Neil Berry struck in five minutes with a header after goalkeeper Gallacher had misjudged a cross from the right. Indeed, the 'keeper was ill at ease on the slippery ground and Clydebank toiled apart from a Treanor shot which was saved admirably by Henry Smith.

A superb left-foot shot from Sandy Clark signalled a second goal in 40 minutes and John Robertson made his contribution seconds from the break by shooting beneath Gallacher's body.

Hearts were able to coast in the second period, quite content to hold their lead until Robertson was fouled by Given in 77 minutes and Black scored a fourth goal. Hughes beat Smith for Clydebank's meagre ration of consolation.

This result took Hearts to within one point of League leaders Aberdeen because there were no other Premier matches played.

Scotland had gone to Australia for a World Cup play-off second leg and any club with a player in the pool were entitled to postpone their fixture.

So it was a great opportunity for Hearts to make headway and to avoid a backlog of fixtures for the closing weeks of the season.

HEARTS: Smith; Kidd, Black; S. Jardine, Berry, Levein; Colquhoun, I. Jardine, Clark, Mackay, Robertson.

CLYDEBANK: Gallacher; Treanor, Given; Maher, Auld, McGhie; Ronald (Hughes), Shanks, Larnach (Conroy), Bain, McCabe.

Referee – D. A. Yeats, Perth.

PREMIER LEAGUE

Hearts	4	Clydebank	1

	P	W	D	L	F	A	Pts
Aberdeen	16	8	5	3	32	15	21
HEARTS	17	8	4	5	26	20	20
Celtic	15	8	3	4	23	17	19
Dundee United	15	7	4	4	23	14	18
Rangers	16	7	3	6	23	18	17
Hibernian	16	6	4	6	25	26	16
St. Mirren	16	7	2	7	23	26	16
Dundee	16	7	1	8	19	27	15
Clydebank	17	3	4	10	15	29	10
Motherwell	16	2	4	10	13	30	8

A deadly twosome — John Robertson and Sandy Clark, both on target against Clydebank

December 7, 1985

Dundee 1, Hearts 1

One of the most exciting games of the season without question. Dundee, who had lost only one of their nine previous championship fixtures with Hearts, threatened to maintain the jinx until Ian Jardine equalised with 10 minutes to go.

Thousands of fans travelled to Dens and saw Hearts set a whirlwind pace. Yet for all their early pressure, Hearts fell behind in seven minutes to an avoidable goal.

Craig Levein fouled Jack on the right and Smith's free kick was pushed out by Henry Smith to the feet of the ever-dangerous Brown who slipped the ball into the net.

Geddes, at the other end, was the hero of the afternoon as he defied Hearts' cleverest shots and he even saved a penalty four minutes from half time. Glennie handled a centre from Gary Mackay but Geddes guessed correctly and dived right to save Kenny Black's shot – his first miss in six spot kicks.

This setback followed a defensive reshuffle when Sandy Jardine had to retire with a leg strain and Brian Whittaker moved from the bench into the left-back role.

Dundee were a cooler bunch in the second half and controlled the game sensibly as Hearts made frantic efforts to draw level.

John Colquhoun had a drive turned onto the crossbar but Dundee were lively, too, and goalkeeper Smith made a smashing save from Stephen.

It was a minute after Dundee had substituted Kidd for Jack that Hearts scored the goal they deserved so much. A free kick from Black was partially cleared and the ball landed at the feet of Ian Jardine who beat Geddes from all of 20 yards with a left-foot shot.

Gary Mackay, a flu victim during the week, went off before the hour, feeling the pace too much for him.

DUNDEE: Geddes; Shannon, Glennie; Rafferty, Smith, Duffy; Stephen, Brown, Harvey, Connor, Jack (Kidd).

HEARTS: Smith; Kidd, Black; S. Jardine (Whittaker), Berry, Levein; Colquhoun, I. Jardine, Clark, Mackay (Watson), Robertson.

Referee – J. Duncan, Gorebridge.

PREMIER LEAGUE

Dundee	1	Hearts	1
Rangers	1	Motherwell	0

	P	W	D	L	F	A	Pts
Aberdeen	16	8	5	3	32	15	21
HEARTS	18	8	5	5	27	21	21
Celtic	15	8	3	4	23	17	19
Rangers	17	8	3	6	24	18	19
Dundee United	15	7	4	4	23	14	18
Hibernian	16	6	4	6	25	26	16
St. Mirren	16	7	2	7	23	26	16
Dundee	17	7	2	8	20	28	16
Clydebank	17	3	4	10	15	29	10
Motherwell	17	2	4	11	13	31	8

December 14, 1985

Hearts 1, Celtic 1

Both clubs wanted to win badly to make ground on Aberdeen and their anxiety was evident in a dogged, slogging match.

A point apiece was probably fair but it meant Celtic were only two points behind Hearts with three games less played.

The game attracted just over 22,000 people and it was exciting enough, especially in the early minutes when Sandy Jardine saved on the goal-line from Johnston after Henry Smith had committed himself.

Jardine, in fact, went on to give a five-star display in defence, unaffected by the swirling wind which appeared to bother many others.

Although they began a little sluggishly, Hearts were in front after nine minutes. John Colquhoun gathered a short corner from Kenny Black and swung over a centre which John Robertson gleefully headed into the net

Slackness in defence almost embarrassed Hearts and yet they almost went two ahead through Ian Jardine who was pipped in an aerial clash by goalkeeper Bonner.

Some heavy tackles were allowed to go unpunished by referee David Syme who, at the time, was in contention for the World Cup appointment which went to Brian McGinlay. It was not one of Mr. Syme's good days.

Smith saved confidently from McGhee and Archdeacon but he was beaten for the equaliser in 66 minutes. McGhee was put through by Johnston and his left footer from 10 yards was a winner.

Hearts replaced Robertson with Andy Watson for the final 15 minutes but they had to be content with a draw when Neil Berry mis-hit a great chance wide of the goal.

HEARTS: Smith; Kidd, Black; S. Jardine, Berry, Levein; Colquhoun, I. Jardine, Clark, Mackay, Robertson (Watson).

CELTIC: Bonner; Grant, Burns; Aitken, McGugan, MacLeod; McClair, P. McStay, McGhee, Johnston, Archdeacon.

Referee – D. F. Syme, Rutherglen.

PREMIER LEAGUE

Aberdeen	4	Hibernian	0
Dundee	3	St. Mirren	1
Hearts	1	Celtic	1
Motherwell	3	Clydebank	0
Rangers	1	Dundee United	1

	P	W	D	L	F	A	Pts
Aberdeen	18	9	5	4	37	17	23
HEARTS	19	8	6	5	28	22	22
Celtic	16	8	4	4	24	18	20
Rangers	18	8	4	6	25	19	20
Dundee United	16	7	5	4	24	15	19
Dundee	18	8	2	8	23	29	18
Hibernian	17	6	4	7	25	30	16
St. Mirren	17	7	2	8	24	29	16
Clydebank	19	4	4	11	17	33	12
Motherwell	18	3	4	11	16	31	10

Dec. 10 — Clydebank 1, Aberdeen 2

December 21, 1985

St. Mirren 0, Hearts 1

Hearts at the top of the Premier League for the first time in the history of the competition was the Christmas gift that every Tynecastle fan welcomed.

In their 12th successive game without defeat, Hearts avenged that Love Street walloping in August and took over the top spot because Aberdeen were beaten by Dundee United.

But this result was not achieved without its controversial moments and St. Mirren manager Alex Miller was reported to the SFA for remarks passed to referee Alistair Huett at the end of the game.

Hearts were awarded a first-half penalty by the Edinburgh official following a foul on Gary Mackay. Kenny Black's first effort was saved but he scored with the rebound.

Then, in injury time, Saints thought they ought to have had a penalty after Cooper had gone down to a tackle by Black. The referee refused their claims and Hearts would have been furious if the spot kick had been given.

So there was a bad-tempered finale to a hard-fought game in which St. Mirren never looked possible winners.

Hearts were much better organised at the back on this visit and it was solid teamwork which took them through. After three away draws, a win was most welcome and extremely significant.

John Robertson and Mackay picked up cautions yet that seemed a small price to pay for the leadership.

John Colquhoun was unwell during the interval and, sensibly, gave way to Andy Watson in the second half. Colin McAdam, fit after his spell Down Under, was on the bench.

ST. MIRREN: Money; Wilson, Abercromby; Rooney (Cameron), Godfrey, Cooper; Fitzpatrick, Winnie, McGarvey, Gallacher (Mackie), Speirs.

HEARTS: Smith; Kidd, Black; S. Jardine, Berry, Levein; Colquhoun (Watson), I. Jardine, Clark, Mackay, Robertson.

Referee – A. Huett, Edinburgh.

Bookings – Mackay, Robertson.

PREMIER LEAGUE

Dundee United	2	Aberdeen	1
Hibernian	1	Rangers	1
St. Mirren	0	Hearts	1

	P	W	D	L	F	A	Pts
HEARTS	20	9	6	5	29	22	24
Aberdeen	19	9	5	5	38	19	23
Dundee United	17	8	5	4	26	16	21
Rangers	19	8	5	6	26	20	21
Celtic	16	8	4	4	24	18	20
Dundee	18	8	2	8	23	29	18
Hibernian	18	6	5	7	26	31	17
St. Mirren	18	7	2	9	24	30	16
Clydebank	19	4	4	11	17	33	12
Motherwell	18	3	4	11	16	31	10

Dec. 17 — Motherwell 3, Clydebank 0

Two barrow-boys at Tynecastle. Alex MacDonald and Sandy Jardine prove that there is more to management than coaching!

December 28, 1985

Rangers 0, Hearts 2

Hearts finished 1985 with the look of potential champions at Ibrox. And thousands of fans streamed from the super stadium convinced that the title could be won.

Only five goals had been conceded while Hearts totted up 21 points from 13 matches and now they had won more games than any of the challengers trailing in their wake.

Rangers had trouble with their undersoil heating and a burst pipe caused the ground staff great anxiety. So it was on a frosty pitch that the well-organised Hearts set about claiming another scalp.

They played it simple and had a prize matchwinner in John Colquhoun, whose darts through the middle punctured an uneasy Rangers defence, unsuited to the conditions.

Colquhoun scored two goals inside 24 minutes and there was no road back for Rangers who could not match the midfield industry of Neil Berry or the solidity of Walter Kidd.

When Hearts moved ahead in 16 minutes, Colquhoun pounced on a mistake by McPherson to thunder a glorious shot past Walker from the edge of the box.

Eight minutes later, a long pass from Ian Jardine had Dawson in a quandary as to where the ball might bounce and Colquhoun was in again to stab home the second goal.

Great opportunities by little John whose double virtually ended the game. Rangers tip tapped in midfield without showing any purpose or penetration and Hearts left them to play away in that manner.

Sandy Clark nearly added a third with a header from Colquhoun's cross and full back Munro appeared on the goal-line to rescue the beaten Walker.

RANGERS: Walker; Dawson, Munro; McPherson, Paterson, Durrant; McCoist, Russell, Nisbet, D. Ferguson, Cooper.

HEARTS: Smith; Kidd, Black; S. Jardine, Berry, Levein; Colquhoun, I. Jardine, Clark, Mackay, Robertson.

Referee – W. P. Knowles, Inverurie.

John Robertson is the lone Heart in this Ibrox picture as he follows up hoping for a mistake by goalkeeper Walker

PREMIER LEAGUE

Clydebank	0	Celtic	2
Dundee United	0	Dundee	0
Rangers	0	Hearts	2

	P	W	D	L	F	A	Pts
HEARTS	21	10	6	5	31	22	26
Dundee United	19	9	6	4	27	16	24
Aberdeen	19	9	5	5	38	19	23
Celtic	18	9	4	5	26	19	22
Dundee	20	8	4	8	23	29	20
Rangers	20	8	5	7	26	22	19
St. Mirren	18	7	2	9	24	30	16
Hibernian	18	6	5	7	26	31	17
Clydebank	21	4	5	12	17	33	13
Motherwell	18	3	4	11	16	31	10

Dec. 23 — Dundee United 1, Celtic 0
Clydebank 0, Dundee 0

January 1, 1986

Hearts 3, Hibernian 1

Although Hearts had been dominating the derby fixture for the past three seasons, they had not won the New Year's Day fixtures at Tynecastle since the days of Conn, Bauld and Wardhaugh in 1955.

This seemed to be the perfect opportunity to put that right, especially with danger-man Durie out of Hibs' team due to suspension.

The pitch which had been frostbound a few days earlier became playable with the arrival of milder weather and the game worked out as most people expected.

Hibs had an early flurry in which Sneddon and Harris almost scored but Hearts were at ease on the muddy surface and played some fine combined football.

Walter Kidd was at his best and Craig Levein took a commanding stand in the middle of the defence to allow their teammates to sweep forward.

With 25 minutes gone, Hearts gained a free kick which John Robertson touched to Ian Jardine and his blockbuster shot went in off Rough's left hand upright.

Hibs charged back in the first 15 minutes of the second half and threatened to make it a lively finish until a burst of goals ended any speculation.

Kenny Black took up terrific position on the right wing after 71 minutes to receive a ball from Walter Kidd. The ball was flashed to the far post where John Robertson was ready to volley the second goal.

Three minutes later, Harris headed Hibs back into the game, yet only for 60 seconds because Sandy Clark scored with a left-foot shot to restore the winning two-goal margin.

Amid this passage, John Colquhoun had an effort saved on the line by Rae as Hearts underlined their greater strength and superiority.

Clark had become the scourge of Hibs since his transfer from Rangers. This was his fifth goal in seven League games against the Easter Road club, a remarkable record of consistency in such a hard-fought fixture.

HEARTS: Smith; Kidd, Black; S. Jardine, Berry, Levein; Colquhoun, I. Jardine, Clark, Mackay, Robertson.

HIBERNIAN: Rough; Sneddon, Brazil; Rae, Fulton, Hunter; Kane, Chisholm, Cowan, Harris, Tortolano (May).

Referee – R. B. Valentine, Dundee.

Sandy Clark and John Robertson celebrate the third goal against Hibs

PREMIER LEAGUE

Celtic	2	Rangers	0
Dundee	0	Aberdeen	0
Hearts	3	Hibernian	1
St. Mirren	3	Clydebank	0

	P	W	D	L	F	A	Pts
HEARTS	22	11	6	5	34	23	28
Aberdeen	20	9	6	5	38	19	24
Dundee United	19	9	6	4	27	16	24
Celtic	19	10	4	5	28	19	24
Rangers	21	8	5	8	26	24	21
Dundee	21	8	5	8	23	29	21
St. Mirren	19	8	2	9	27	30	18
Hibernian	19	6	5	8	27	34	17
Clydebank	22	4	5	13	17	38	13
Motherwell	18	3	4	11	16	31	10

January 4, 1986

Motherwell 1, Hearts 3

Lines were obliterated by falling snow and the Fir Park groundstaff worked quickly to re-mark them before the kick off.

Underneath the snow, the park was hard and frostbound which resulted in dreadful conditions. Indeed, there seemed a doubt whether the game would be finished.

However, the wintry blast couldn't halt Hearts who made a valiant second-half comeback to satisfy a travelling support of some 7000 fans.

It was all a matter of trying to stay upright and the pitch was a great leveller. Motherwell had plenty enthusiasm and Wright caused a few anxious moments before they took the lead eight minutes from half time.

McStay reached Reilly with a throw-in and the centre forward turned smartly to fire a left-foot shot past Smith from the edge of the penalty box.

Hearts had to forget the snow and go for goals to avoid a second defeat at the ground and, within 10 minutes of the second half, they were on course for victory.

Full back MacLeod left a passback woefully short and Ian Jardine took full advantage to slip home the equaliser. That was the spur Hearts needed and Motherwell found themselves trailing two minutes later.

Non-stop pressure unsettled the home defence and Neil Berry benefited from the work of John Robertson and Sandy Clark to score from close in.

Motherwell were up against it and the switch of Blair for Dornan did not alter the trend. Hearts were in command and Colin McAdam made his first team debut after 81 minutes as replacement for John Colquhoun.

Five minutes from the end, Robbo added a third goal following a free kick and Hearts had proved they were capable of coming from behind to win.

MOTHERWELL: Gardiner; Wishart, MacLeod; Doyle, McCart, Boyd; Dornan (Blair), McStay, Reilly, Wright, Mulvaney.

HEARTS: Smith; Kidd, Black; S. Jardine, Berry, Levein; Colquhoun (McAdam), I. Jardine, Clark, Mackay, Robertson.

Referee – K. O'Donnell, Airdrie.

PREMIER LEAGUE

Aberdeen	3	St. Mirren	1
Dundee United	4	Celtic	2
Hibernian	2	Clydebank	3
Motherwell	1	Hearts	3
Rangers	5	Dundee	0

	P	W	D	L	F	A	Pts
HEARTS	23	12	6	5	37	24	30
Aberdeen	21	10	6	5	41	20	26
Dundee United	20	10	6	4	31	18	26
Celtic	20	10	4	6	30	23	24
Rangers	22	9	5	8	31	24	23
Dundee	22	8	5	9	23	34	21
St. Mirren	20	8	2	10	28	33	18
Hibernian	20	6	5	9	29	37	17
Clydebank	23	5	5	13	20	40	15
Motherwell	19	3	4	12	17	34	10

January 11, 1986

Hearts 1, Dundee United 1

A back injury sustained in training forced Ian Jardine to miss this game so Hearts made their first change in nine matches with Brian Whittaker restored to the defence.

Thunder and lightning before the kick off could not undermine the enthusiasm of the fans and 19,000 customers refused to give the bad weather a second thought.

United had gone 10 matches without loss and were looming up as serious contenders for the title. It was imperative, therefore, to thwart their challenge.

Hearts started promisingly and Hegarty blocked a netbound effort from Neil Berry before John Colquhoun sent one wide and goalkeeper Thomson had to kick clear twice.

It was good stuff and Bannon nearly laid on a goal for Sturrock whose rising header cleared the crossbar. Just one minute from half time, Hearts were handed a glorious chance to score from a penalty.

Paul Hegarty rescues Dundee United after goalkeeper Billy Thomson was beaten by Neil Berry's shot. John Robertson has his arms raised to salute a goal

Gary Mackay was fouled by Gallacher and took the kick himself. Thomson read the script perfectly and dived left to stop a modest shot.

Gary made the fans forget that boob with a fine goal in 63 minutes. Sandy Clark headed down a pass from Berry and Mackay steered a 15 yarder into the net.

Hearts' joy was shortlived for United hit back within six minutes. Craig Levein diverted a Dodds cross to Bannon who smashed a terrific left-footed volley past Henry Smith from the left side of the box.

Coyne, who had come on as a replacement for Redford soon after half time, started to trouble the home defence and United had their slickest spell in the last 20 minutes.

Hearts were content with a draw which gave them 19 points from 12 matches. In the first third of their fixtures, the team had collected only 12 points, or one per outing.

The improvement was obvious and the squad set off for a holiday in Marbella content with their lot, particularly Mackay and Clark who had played splendidly.

HEARTS: Smith; Kidd, Whittaker; S. Jardine, Berry, Levein; Colquhoun, Black, Clark, Mackay, Robertson.

DUNDEE UNITED: Thomson; Malpas, Beaumont; Gough, Hegarty, Narey; Bannon, Gallacher, Redford (Coyne), Sturrock, Dodds.

Referee – D. McVicar, Carluke.

PREMIER LEAGUE

Celtic	1	Aberdeen	1
Rangers	4	Clydebank	2
Dundee	3	Hibernian	1
Hearts	1	Dundee United	1
St. Mirren	1	Motherwell	0

	P	W	D	L	F	A	Pts
HEARTS	24	12	7	5	38	25	31
Aberdeen	22	10	7	5	42	21	27
Dundee United	21	10	7	4	32	19	27
Celtic	21	10	5	6	31	24	25
Rangers	23	10	5	8	35	26	25
Dundee	23	9	5	9	26	35	23
St. Mirren	21	9	2	10	29	33	20
Hibernian	21	6	5	10	30	40	17
Clydebank	24	5	5	14	22	44	15
Motherwell	20	3	4	13	17	35	10

January 18, 1986

Aberdeen 0, Hearts 1

Champions Aberdeen, almost invincible on their own Pittodrie, were beaten at home for the first time in 13 months. It was a great victory for Hearts in their campaign for the championship and the truth is they never looked in danger of defeat.

Six points separated the clubs following this hard-fought duel and Alex Ferguson, the Aberdeen boss, suggested Dundee United would win the League as the gleeful Hearts players climbed aboard their coach with other thoughts.

Aberdeen, minus the banned Cooper, were kicking themselves over an early miss by Black. Henry Smith blocked his original shot and the Under 21 cap was so casual in meeting the rebound from a few yards that Sandy Jardine was able to make a goal-line save.

Everyone was in a tearing hurry but the grey-shirted Hearts looked formidable and they shrugged aside a few refereeing decisions which were debatable.

In fact, Leighton had a magnificent save from Ian Jardine whose shot was pushed against the post and Hearts had an unbelievable miss three minutes from half time.

Gary Mackay bemused the Dons defence with a mazy run and left Sandy Clark to finish the move. He cracked the ball against the bar and it fell perfectly for him to score at the second attempt. Amazingly, the ball slid off the side of his boot and the seemingly helpless Leighton was able to grab it.

A draw appeared certain until Hearts substituted Colin McAdam for John Robertson in 82 minutes. It might have been interpreted as a negative move but manager MacDonald wanted the big man to compete with Aberdeen's tall defenders.

It was a ruse that worked ideally because John Colquhoun found a gap in 84 minutes to smash a right-foot drive past Leighton.

Aberdeen had nothing left with which to retaliate and a big travelling support roared their approval of a vital victory.

ABERDEEN: Leighton; McKimmie, McQueen (Mitchell); Stark, McLeish, W. Miller; Black, Simpson, McDougall (J. Miller), Bett, Weir.

HEARTS: Smith; Kidd, Black; S. Jardine, Berry, Levein; Colquhoun, I. Jardine, Clark, Mackay, Robertson (McAdam).

Referee – J. McCluskey, Stewarton.

Bookings – Levein, I. Jardine, Kidd, McAdam.

PREMIER LEAGUE

Aberdeen	0	Hearts	1
Dundee United	4	Clydebank	0
Hibernian	2	Celtic	2
Motherwell	2	Dundee	2
Rangers	2	St. Mirren	0

	P	W	D	L	F	A	Pts
HEARTS	25	13	7	5	39	25	33
Dundee United	22	11	7	4	36	19	29
Celtic	23	11	6	6	36	28	28
Aberdeen	23	10	7	6	42	22	27
Rangers	24	11	5	8	37	26	27
Dundee	24	9	6	9	28	37	24
St. Mirren	22	9	2	11	29	35	20
Hibernian	22	6	6	10	32	42	18
Clydebank	25	5	5	15	22	48	15
Motherwell	22	3	5	14	21	40	11

Jan. 15 — Celtic 3, Motherwell 2

February 1, 1986

Clydebank 1, Hearts 1

Hearts were given a huge scare by the struggling Bankies who made it a very physical contest and had to play with 10 men for 45 minutes after left back Given had been sent off at the start of the second half.

Every member of the Clydebank back four was booked in the first half for their rugged approach and it was evident they would be lucky to keep a full team on the park.

Nevertheless, Hearts toiled to develop any rhythm and appeared to be heading for defeat when Sandy Clark snatched the equaliser with three minutes left.

So it was their dogged, never-say-die spirit which allowed Hearts to stay four points clear of the field, having played all their Premier rivals twice since embarking on a long undefeated sequence.

Roddy McDonald returned to the Tynecastle back division for the first time since September as the stand-in for the suspended Craig Levein.

Clydebank fought doggedly in midfield and Neil Berry never stopped running in an effort to combat them.

Hearts made a mini-shuffle after the break with Colin McAdam on in place of Ian Jardine and Clydebank introduced Maher soon after the departure of Given for a foul on Walter Kidd.

Despite being a man short, Clydebank scored in 51 minutes and that was a shock for Hearts. Poor defensive play cost the goal as Shanks moved through unchallenged to shoot past Henry Smith from 10 yards.

Clydebank were annoyed that no penalty was forthcoming as Smith brought down Gibson in the box and Hearts picked up bookings as their frustration grew.

However, it was a happier sign that Gallacher had to save expertly to stop an equalising try from Berry, and Sandy Clark salvaged a point with his late and valuable strike.

CLYDEBANK: Gallacher; Dickson, Given; Fallon, Auld, Treanor; Shanks, Gibson, Larnach (Maher), Lloyd, McCabe.

HEARTS: Smith; Kidd, Black; S. Jardine, Berry, McDonald; Colquhoun, I. Jardine (McAdam), Clark, Mackay, Robertson.

Referee – I. Cathcart, Bridge of Allan.

Bookings – McAdam, McDonald.

PREMIER LEAGUE

Clydebank	1	Hearts	1
Dundee	1	Celtic	3
Hibernian	4	Motherwell	0
Rangers	1	Aberdeen	1
St. Mirren	1	Dundee United	1

	P	W	D	L	F	A	Pts
HEARTS	26	13	8	5	40	26	34
Dundee United	23	11	8	4	37	20	30
Celtic	24	12	6	6	39	29	30
Aberdeen	24	10	8	6	43	23	28
Rangers	25	11	6	8	38	27	28
Dundee	25	9	6	10	29	40	24
St. Mirren	23	9	3	11	30	36	21
Hibernian	23	7	6	10	36	42	20
Clydebank	26	5	6	15	23	49	16
Motherwell	23	3	5	15	21	44	11

February 8, 1986

Hearts 3, Dundee 1

Hearts cleared the pitch of snow and had a lucky break when the frost that was forecast did not materialise.

Ian Jardine was out with a groin strain and Craig Levein was completing his two-match ban which meant Hearts had to spar cautiously against dangerous rivals.

The scene was far from happy after 10 minutes, for Henry Smith dropped a cross from McKinlay at the feet of newcomer Mennie who could scarcely believe his good luck.

However, Hearts were handed an ideal opportunity to nullify that goal in 20 minutes. Glennie hauled down Sandy Clark in the box but, to the anguish of players and fans alike, John Colquhoun struck a poor penalty which Geddes saved.

Two minutes later, though, Colquhoun put things right by heading in a centre from Black while Dundee shouted in vain for an offside decision.

Dundee suffered a setback close to half time when their menacing midfield player, Brown, was hurt and replaced by McCormack.

Hearts were over their nervous start and moved ahead in 59 minutes with a 12 yarder from John Robertson following neat play between Brian Whittaker, Colquhoun and Robbo.

Now there was only one winner. Gary Mackay danced past three defenders to clip a gorgeous third goal in 68 minutes and Dundee's frustration was reflected in the departure of Glennie in 84 minutes for his second bookable offence.

There was good cause for Hearts to celebrate this success as it was their first win at home against Dundee in the Premier League since March, 1976.

HEARTS: Smith; Kidd, Black; S. Jardine, Berry, McDonald; Colquhoun, Whittaker, Clark, Mackay, Robertson.

DUNDEE: Geddes; Glennie, McKinlay; Forsyth, Smith, Duffy; Hendrie, Brown (McCormack), Mennie, Connor, Harvey.

Referee – D. Yeats, Perth.

Sandy Jardine and Walter Kidd are on hand as Henry Smith punches clear from Dundee's Graham Harvey

PREMIER LEAGUE

Aberdeen	4	Clydebank	1
Celtic	1	St. Mirren	1
Dundee United	4	Hibernian	0
Hearts	3	Dundee	1
Motherwell	1	Rangers	0

	P	W	D	L	F	A	Pts
HEARTS	27	14	8	5	43	27	36
Dundee United	24	12	8	4	41	20	32
Celtic	25	12	7	6	40	30	31
Aberdeen	25	11	8	6	47	24	30
Rangers	26	11	6	9	38	28	28
Dundee	26	9	6	11	30	43	24
St. Mirren	24	9	4	11	31	37	22
Hibernian	24	7	6	11	36	46	20
Clydebank	27	5	6	16	24	53	16
Motherwell	24	4	5	15	22	44	13

February 22, 1986

Celtic 1, Hearts 1

This was supposed to be Celtic's big chance to cut into the five points advantage Hearts held over them but the Tynecastle side kept their lead intact by forcing a draw.

Five points off Celtic was a handsome haul and it was John Robertson's 13th League goal of the season which proved unlucky for the Parkhead club.

Craig Levein returned to the defence after serving a two-match suspension which had allowed him the opportunity to spend a few days in the Portuguese sun.

Celtic, on the other hand, were beset by team problems. Bonner, Grant and Paul McStay were unfit and manager Hay gambled on the fitness of MacLeod in midfield. Still, he put together a fighting squad with youth cap Whyte at full back and Aitken in midfield.

They compensated for a shortage of class with a gutsy display and a 45,000 crowd created a super atmosphere for such an important game.

Hearts were put under pressure as Aitken tried to control the play and one wholehearted run forced Henry Smith to dive at his feet.

Referee Ferguson had a rebuke for manager Alex MacDonald in the dug-out following a protest over a tackle by Burns on Ian Jardine but there was more to concern the boss once Celtic snapped ahead on the half hour.

Hearts might have expected Levein or Sandy Jardine to clear a ball from McClair but, as they dallied, Johnston cracked the ball past Smith.

It was a huge bonus for Hearts to equalise in 44 minutes with their first genuine chance. Sandy Clark nodded down a pass from Ian Jardine and Robbo rifled a right footer behind Latchford.

Hearts had a better second half, though a gallant right-wing run by Aitken against all the odds presented McGhee with a chance he fluffed. In the closing minutes, Hearts gave a debut chance to Billy McKay as substitute for John Robertson. Quite a stage for his comeback to top football after his career seemed to be over.

CELTIC: Latchford; W. McStay, McGrain; Aitken, McGugan, MacLeod; McClair, McGhee (Shepherd), Johnston, Whyte, Burns.

HEARTS: Smith; Kidd, Black; S. Jardine, Berry, Levein; Colquhoun, I. Jardine, Clark, Mackay, Robertson (McKay).

Referee – A. Ferguson, Giffnock.

Bookings – I. Jardine, Berry.

Tommy Burns and Ian Jardine in a private duel at Parkhead

PREMIER LEAGUE

Celtic	1	Hearts	1
Dundee United	1	Rangers	1
Hibernian	0	Aberdeen	1
St. Mirren	1	Dundee	2

	P	W	D	L	F	A	Pts
HEARTS	28	14	9	5	44	28	37
Aberdeen	27	13	8	6	49	24	34
Dundee United	25	12	9	4	42	21	33
Celtic	26	12	8	6	41	31	32
Rangers	28	11	7	10	39	30	29
Dundee	27	10	6	11	32	44	26
St. Mirren	25	9	4	12	32	39	22
Hibernian	25	7	6	12	36	47	20
Clydebank	27	5	6	16	24	53	16
Motherwell	24	4	5	15	22	44	13

Feb. 19 — Aberdeen 1, Rangers 0

March 15, 1986

Hearts 2, Motherwell 0

Motherwell arrived in great heart having beaten Dundee United in midweek and learned that the modifications in the League structure would mean no relegation at the end of the season.

So it threatened to be a much harder fixture than it looked on paper and Motherwell competed solidly in the first half hour.

In fact, the best chance fell to Reilly and it needed both quick thinking and fast action from Henry Smith to block his shot.

Suddenly, the pressure was lifted in the space of six minutes. Roddy McDonald, recalled to the defence in place of the injured Sandy Jardine, joined his attack for a corner and Kenny Black's inswinging cross from the right was headed into the net off Murray's body.

That breakthrough helped to relax the players and when John Colquhoun was fouled in the box after 38 minutes, John Robertson calmly stuck away his second penalty in seven days to banish the memory of spot kicks missed earlier in the season.

Apart from another good save by Smith from substitute Blair, Hearts were very much in command in the second half.

Robertson went off with 20 minutes left to save aggravating a knock on the thigh and Billy McKay had another brief appearance.

What made the result so important was the news from elsewhere. Celtic and Dundee United both dropped a point in their Parkhead draw and Aberdeen failed to win at Paisley. Hearts were firmly in the driving seat and able to win the championship without any outside assistance.

HEARTS: Smith; Kidd, Black; McDonald, Berry, Levein; Colquhoun, Whittaker, Clark, Mackay, Robertson (W. McKay).

MOTHERWELL: Gardiner; Wishart, Murray; Doyle, Forbes (Harrow), Boyd; Baptie, MacLeod, Reilly, Wright (Blair), Walker.

Referee – D. F. Syme, Rutherglen.

All eyes on the ball as Roddy McDonald and Craig Levein go looking for a goal against Motherwell

PREMIER LEAGUE

Celtic	1	Dundee United	1
Clydebank	1	Hibernian	3
Dundee	2	Rangers	1
Hearts	2	Motherwell	0
St. Mirren	1	Aberdeen	1

	P	W	D	L	F	A	Pts
HEARTS	29	15	9	5	46	28	39
Dundee United	28	13	10	5	44	24	36
Aberdeen	28	13	9	6	50	25	35
Celtic	27	12	9	6	42	32	33
Rangers	30	12	7	11	43	33	31
Dundee	29	12	6	11	38	45	30
Hibernian	29	9	6	14	43	52	24
St. Mirren	27	9	5	13	33	43	23
Clydebank	29	5	6	18	25	60	16
Motherwell	26	5	5	16	24	46	15

Mar. 1 — Dundee 4, Clydebank 0
Rangers 3, Hibernian 1
Mar. 12 — Motherwell 2, Dundee United 0
Hibernian 3, St. Mirren 0

March 22, 1986

Hibernian 1, Hearts 2

There were plenty of reasons for the large contingent of Hearts fans to celebrate after this latest derby triumph. Firstly, there was the new Premier League record of 22 games without defeat and a haul of seven points from Hibs in the four local clashes.

Indeed, it was the first time since the start of the 10-team competition in 1975 that Hearts could claim to be ahead of Hibs in the points score.

With 24 games played between the clubs, Hearts had taken 25 points to 23, having won six and drawn six in the past three seasons.

A howling gale made conditions difficult for the players and so it was in no way a classic. The tackling was swift and hard to such an extent that Gorebridge referee Jimmy Duncan had six names in his book by half time.

Craig Levein and Gary Mackay were the Tynecastle victims in a punishing 45 minutes but there was the consolation of a half time lead obtained by Sandy Clark seven minutes from the interval.

Hearts forced two corners and the second one was cleared only as far as Walter Kidd who hoisted the ball back into the goalmouth. Hibs defenders were charging out to play the Hearts forwards offside but Clark fastened onto the ball and slid it past Rough.

Sandy Jardine, back in the side after a calf strain, was a calming influence in the second half when Hearts faced the wind and Henry Smith gripped two rasping corners from Tortolano in brilliant style.

Hibs equalised in 64 minutes with a fine header by Cowan from a Tortolano free kick but the game was level for just two minutes.

Milne used his hand to keep out a scoring header from John Robertson and the little striker fired home his third spot kick in successive games to win the points. That goal was Robbo's 20th of the season and his eighth in the last eight matches. Neil Berry suffered a black eye in a clash of heads with Fulton.

HIBERNIAN: Rough; Sneddon, Milne; May, Fulton, Hunter (Rae); Collins, Chisholm, Cowan, Durie (Harris), Tortolano.

HEARTS: Smith; Kidd, Black; S. Jardine, Berry, Levein; Colquhoun, Whittaker, Clark, Mackay, Robertson.

Referee – J. Duncan, Gorebridge.

Bookings – Levein, Mackay.

Kenny Black and Sandy Jardine have a 2-1 advantage over Steve Cowan, of Hibs

PREMIER LEAGUE

Aberdeen	0	Dundee	0
Clydebank	0	St. Mirren	2
Dundee United	4	Motherwell	0
Hibernian	1	Hearts	2
Rangers	4	Celtic	4

	P	W	D	L	F	A	Pts
HEARTS	30	16	9	5	48	29	41
Dundee United	29	14	10	5	48	24	38
Aberdeen	29	13	10	6	50	25	36
Celtic	28	12	10	6	46	36	34
Rangers	31	12	8	11	47	37	32
Dundee	30	12	7	11	38	45	31
St. Mirren	28	10	5	13	35	43	25
Hibernian	31	9	6	16	44	56	24
Motherwell	28	6	5	17	26	50	17
Clydebank	30	5	6	19	25	62	16

Mar. 18 — Motherwell 2, Hibernian 0

March 25, 1986

Hearts 3, St. Mirren 0

It was quite unusual for Hearts to be involved in a championship game in midweek after maintaining their schedule through the worst of the winter. This fixture was the only casualty and Hearts used it to surge five points clear with five matches left.

Of course, Dundee United had two matches in hand but it was a handsome lead at such a late stage in the season.

Hearts made a mockery of the form in their first disastrous duel at Paisley when they conceded six goals. For this was their fourth straight win against Saints, including a cup tie, with a scoreline of 11-1.

They won very comfortably in the end but had one bad scare in the first half. St. Mirren forward Gallacher was put through with Henry Smith to beat and hammered the ball over the bar from 12 yards.

Hearts were relieved to keep the scoresheet blank at that early juncture and there was relief coupled with joy once Craig Levein moved into attack to head his second League goal. He outjumped everyone in the box to steer home a corner from Kenny Black, who had shown up better than most in the packed midfield area.

While manager Alex MacDonald stressed afterwards that the players were not suffering from title nerves, the team played in a more relaxed fashion with a goal to their credit.

It was even better when John Robertson backheeled the second goal in a crowded six yards box 20 minutes from the end. In 86 minutes, Sandy Clark headed the third goal from another centre by Black.

So Hearts had scored their first half-century in the Premier League and topped 40 points for the first time. John Colquhoun was limping as the team went off to a standing ovation from more than 13,000 happy fans.

The only black spot on the evening was a booking for Walter Kidd whose penalty points jumped into double figures and meant a three-match ban in April.

HEARTS: Smith; Kidd, Whittaker; S. Jardine, Berry, Levein; Colquhoun, Black, Clark, Mackay, Robertson.

ST. MIRREN: Money; D. Hamilton, Clarke; Rooney, Godfrey, Cooper; B. Hamilton, Winnie, McGarvey, Gallacher (McDowall), Speirs.

Referee – K. O'Donnell, Airdrie.

Booking – Kidd.

PREMIER LEAGUE

	P	W	D	L	F	A	Pts
HEARTS	31	17	9	5	51	29	43
Dundee United	29	14	10	5	48	24	38
Aberdeen	29	13	10	6	50	25	36
Celtic	28	12	10	6	46	36	34
Rangers	31	12	8	11	47	37	32
Dundee	30	12	7	11	38	45	31
St. Mirren	29	10	5	14	35	46	25
Hibernian	31	9	6	16	44	56	24
Motherwell	28	6	5	17	26	50	17
Clydebank	30	5	6	19	25	62	16

March 29, 1986

Hearts 3, Rangers 1

Two more goals for the lethal-finishing John Robertson gunned down Rangers for the fourth time this season – in itself a feat to cherish.

It was the sixth successive championship game in which Robbo had been on the mark and he brought his total to five in matches against Rangers this season.

There was a five-minute delay at the start as close on 25,000 fans poured into the ground and Hearts did not disappoint their supporters by extending their unbeaten League run to 24 matches.

With eight minutes gone, Kenny Black chipped the ball forward for Robbo who supplied his own delicate lob to beat goalkeeper Walker.

Apart from a disallowed goal by McCoist, Hearts were comfortable leaders to the break and Robertson added his second goal from a penalty in 47 minutes. McKinnon handled a Sandy Clark header on the line but Rangers complained that the free kick which led to the incident was unfair.

McKinnon, Durrant and Fraser were booked as Rangers tried desperately hard to recover and McCoist made it 2-1 from a penalty kick in 66 minutes after he had been bumped by Clark. Straight away Ian Jardine took over from Gary Mackay, for whom this was his 200th appearance for Hearts.

That goal was the signal for Hearts to become uneasy and they seemed to fret that Rangers might salvage a point in the final phase.

Cooper and Russell were introduced with that target in mind but Hearts resisted their pressure and secured a third goal in injury time.

John Robertson follows his neat lob into the net for the first goal against Rangers with Munro and Walker helpless

It followed the substitution of Colin McAdam for John Colquhoun and Clark, minus one boot, took the kudos as he slipped home a pass from Robertson.

HEARTS: Smith; Kidd, Whittaker; S. Jardine, Berry, Levein; Colquhoun (McAdam), Black, Clark, Mackay (I. Jardine), Robertson.

RANGERS: Walker; Burns, Munro; McPherson, McKinnon, Durrant; McMinn, Fraser, Fleck (Cooper), Bell (Russell), McCoist.

Referee – H. Alexander, Kilmarnock.

A diving clearance from Walter Kidd prevents Rangers' McMinn from making contact with the ball. Ally McCoist awaits developments

PREMIER LEAGUE

Clydebank	0	Celtic	5
Dundee	0	Dundee United	1
Hearts	3	Rangers	1
Motherwell	0	Aberdeen	1
St. Mirren	0	Hibernian	2

	P	W	D	L	F	A	Pts
HEARTS	32	18	9	5	54	30	45
Dundee United	30	15	10	5	49	24	40
Aberdeen	30	14	10	6	51	25	38
Celtic	29	13	10	6	51	36	36
Rangers	32	12	8	12	48	40	32
Dundee	31	12	7	12	38	46	31
Hibernian	32	10	6	16	46	56	26
St. Mirren	30	10	5	15	35	48	25
Motherwell	29	6	5	18	26	51	17
Clydebank	31	5	6	20	25	67	16

April 12, 1986

Dundee United 0, Hearts 3

This was the day Hearts tied up the championship with a crushing defeat of the team that had seemed most likely to upset their ambitions. Unbeaten at Tannadice in League football for 18 months, United felt they could win and go on to the title.

But they were swept away by a maroon avalanche after John Robertson hit one of the best goals he'll ever score to give Hearts a first half lead.

With 24 minutes to go, a dejected Dundee side trailed by three goals and nobody had to tell them that Hearts had shattered their two trophy hopes in the space of eight days.

Yet another all-ticket occasion was necessary and Hearts used up every ticket in their 7000 allocation for what many pundits claimed could be a championship decider.

Hearts had George Cowie at right back for the first time since September with Walter Kidd banned for three matches and he played with the calmness of a regular member.

United went on attack from the first minute, anxious that Hearts should be denied the initiative. But their high crosses into goal were less than subtle and the pressure was fairly harmless, if constant.

Hearts delivered their body blow in 24 minutes with an action replay of their semi final goal except it was Robbo who supplied the exquisite finish when Hegarty headed out a lob from Craig Levein.

John took the ball left footed on the half volley from 20 yards and it was only a blur to goalkeeper Thomson as it crashed into his right hand corner. What a goal and what a fillip for Hearts!

Meanwhile, Sandy Clark covered every yard of the park, attacking one minute and then back-checking to compete against Gough or Hegarty when they moved into attack. His contribution was immense and demanded great stamina.

Once it was all over, United boss Jim McLean admitted that he had given up hope once Henry Smith brought off a marvellous diving save from Malpas. The goalkeeper threw himself to the right and stretched out an arm to push the ball aside after the defender had made perfect contact with a rebound off Bannon's free kick.

That would have been the equaliser but Smith was in invincible mood, having predicted "It's my lucky day" in the Swallow Hotel where Hearts had their pre-match meal. What prompted the thought was his consistent

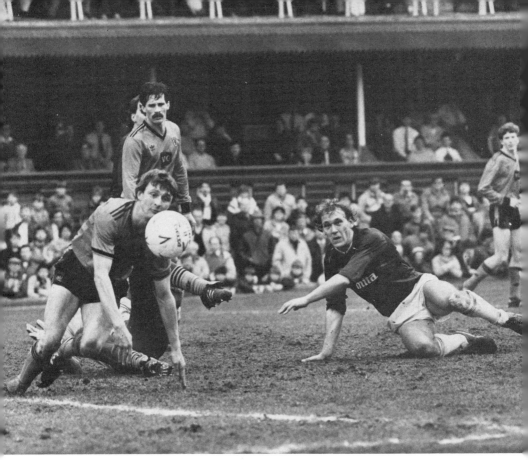

Hegarty, Dundee United, clears a header from Sandy Clark

collection from the one-armed bandit which gurgled out its own bonus.

With 58 minutes played, Neil Berry swung over a long cross from the right, John Colquhoun headed the ball into the middle from beyond the far post and Clark poked it home.

Hearts were out on their own, United out on their feet and Robbo pounced on a slick pass from Colquhoun to dribble past Thomson for number three in 66 minutes.

United brought on two substitutes and Hearts introduced Colin McAdam for Gary Mackay to sit in front of the back four in a gesture of consolidation. Four games against United had yielded six points – not to mention the Cup result.

DUNDEE UNITED: Thomson, Malpas, Holt, Gough, Hegarty, Narey, Bannon (Clark), Gallacher, Beedie, Sturrock, Dodds (Redford).

HEARTS: Smith, Cowie, Whittaker, S. Jardine, Berry, Levein, Colquhoun, Black, Clark, Mackay (McAdam), Robertson.

Referee – K. J. Hope, Clarkston.

68

Gary Mackay in a race for the ball at Tannadice

PREMIER LEAGUE

Aberdeen	0	Celtic	1
Clydebank	2	Rangers	1
Dundee United	0	Hearts	3
Hibernian	1	Dundee	0
Motherwell	1	St. Mirren	2

	P	W	D	L	F	A	Pts
HEARTS	33	19	9	5	57	30	47
Dundee United	32	16	10	6	54	27	42
Celtic	32	16	10	6	56	38	42
Aberdeen	32	15	10	7	54	28	40
Rangers	33	12	8	13	49	42	32
Dundee	33	12	7	14	39	49	31
Hibernian	33	11	6	16	47	56	28
St. Mirren	33	11	5	17	38	56	27
Clydebank	33	6	7	20	28	69	19
Motherwell	32	6	6	20	30	57	18

Apr. 2 — Celtic 2, Dundee 1
Apr. 5 — St. Mirren 1, Celtic 2
            Clydebank 1, Motherwell 1
Apr. 8 — Dundee United 5, St. Mirren 0
Apr. 9 — Aberdeen 3, Motherwell 2

April 20, 1986

Hearts 1, Aberdeen 1

Scotland's first League game to be screened live on television almost spelled the end of Hearts' marvellous run, for John Colquhoun had to produce an equaliser with only three minutes left.

The roar of joy and relief might have been heard at Pittodrie since it must be said that Hearts hadn't looked like saving the game.

They were upset at being forced to play on a Sunday and the players and management team made it clear that they deplored the switch from Saturday.

At least, the fans did not stay at home and the attendance of more than 19,000 created a suitable atmosphere. Yet Hearts were out of sorts, nervous and fidgety, and not a patch on the team which had surged away from their pursuers.

The strain was obvious and the carefree Aberdeen players approached the game purposefully and with no real worries about the result.

Hearts were too often second to the ball, gave it away carelessly, and the majority of the players on both sides seemed to want to play in the middle third of the pitch which resulted in terrible bunching.

It could not have been gripping entertainment for the viewers, though Aberdeen, spurred by the smooth distribution of McMaster, were the better team.

Hewitt and Joe Miller missed chances in the first half and all Hearts offered in reply was a left-foot shot from Sandy Clark which Gunn smothered at his right-hand post.

A couple of astonishingly cool passbacks by Kenny Black, while under intense pressure, won applause from a jittery audience but Hearts were unable to put their act together. Neither was referee Bob Valentine who gave a series of unpopular decisions.

Hearts substituted Ian Jardine for Gary Mackay in 65 minutes and Aberdeen countered this move by calling in Eric Black.

In the circumstances, Hearts would have settled for a goalless draw especially when Kenny Black underlined their nervous state by hitting a right-wing corner into the sidenet.

Fifteen minutes from time, Aberdeen were given a disputed penalty. Was a Willie Miller lob handled by both Bett and Ian Jardine or just the Hearts man? The referee took the latter view and Weir scored with the kick.

Jubilation for Hearts players and fans after Colquhoun scored to equalise against Aberdeen at Tynecastle

Five minutes later, McLeish could have been ordered off for hauling down John Colquhoun after the little forward had left him leaden footed. Another booking was no consolation to Hearts and the 'professional foul' went unpunished by a poor referee.

However, the best moment was still to come for Hearts. John Robertson jostled for possession of a loose ball which broke kindly and jet-paced John Colquhoun burst in to poke the ball behind Gunn. A Houdini act without doubt and Hearts acknowledged the fact that they had returned from the dead to stay three points in front.

HEARTS: Smith; Cowie, Whittaker; S. Jardine, Berry, Levein; Colquhoun, Black, Clark, Mackay (I. Jardine), Robertson.

ABERDEEN: Gunn; McKimmie, McQueen; McMaster, McLeish, W. Miller; Hewitt (Black), Mitchell (Robertson), J. Miller, Bett, Weir.

Referee — R. B. Valentine, Dundee.

PREMIER LEAGUE

Celtic	2	Hibernian	0
Clydebank	1	Dundee United	1
Dundee	4	Motherwell	0
St. Mirren	2	Rangers	1

	P	W	D	L	F	A	Pts
HEARTS	34	19	10	5	58	31	48
Dundee United	34	17	11	6	56	28	45
Celtic	33	17	10	6	58	38	44
Aberdeen	34	15	11	8	55	30	41
Dundee	34	13	7	14	43	49	33
Rangers	34	12	8	14	50	44	32
St. Mirren	34	12	5	17	40	57	29
Hibernian	34	11	6	17	47	58	28
Clydebank	34	6	8	20	29	70	20
Motherwell	33	6	6	21	30	61	18

Apr. 16 — Aberdeen 0, Dundee United 1
Apr. 20 — Hearts 1, Aberdeen 1

April 26, 1986

Hearts 1, Clydebank 0

Hearts decided to accommodate any Clydebank followers in the stand and to open up the Gorgie Road end of the ground to their own fans to ensure there would be ample room. Just over 20,000 turned out hoping to hail the new champions.

But, at the end of a nervous 90 minutes, the championship remained undecided. Hearts had increased their score to 50 points which only Celtic could equal by defeating Motherwell in midweek and St. Mirren on Saturday.

In a nutshell, Hearts had to gain one point in their last match at Dundee or risk a decision on goal difference which was too close for comfort.

This game against Clydebank turned into a tense pressure pot and over-anxiety among the players was evident from start to finish.

For the second time in a week, Hearts did not do themselves justice and the cavalier spirit was absent as they struggled to victory.

Hearts' only ploy was to hit high balls through the middle to Sandy Clark who had a rugged and able rival in Auld. Not enough use was made of the wings and the Bankies retreated in strength to deny the home side any room.

McCabe, in midfield, showed tidy ball control and he caused a few unsettling moments in defence. On the whole, however, Hearts were in command and never looked likely to lose.

Kenny Black, who was replaced by Ian Jardine in the second half, and Sandy Clark were not at their sharpest and it's possible they had in mind the fact that a booking would have put them out of the Cup final a fortnight later.

Goalkeeper Gallacher had a smart early save from Clark following a four man move and Clydebank were not in the market for a heavy defeat. Conroy was booked for a heavy tackle on Cowie which underlined their determination.

John Colquhoun was the liveliest forward without benefiting from the right service and it needed a flash of inspiration to score what proved to be the winner.

Sandy Jardine and George Cowie worked a neat one-two out of defence and Gary Mackay picked up the ball around the halfway line after 34 minutes. He built up speed, eased past a couple of defenders and smashed a left footer high into the net from 18 yards.

A terrific goal and the fans chanted their approval in anticipation of a few more. But it was a case for consolidation first and wait for the Bankies to tire.

Both sides introduced a new face for the last 20 minutes and John Robertson, who had been strangely quiet, almost scored in the closing minutes.

Gallacher stopped a right-foot shot from him and then Mackay threaded a brilliant pass behind the Clydebank defence. Robertson tried to slide it past Gallacher on the ground but the goalkeeper blocked it and John couldn't turn the ball in from a terrible angle wide of the right-hand post.

So Hearts had completed their 18 home fixtures without loss and kept an early season promise that they would be hard to beat at Tynecastle.

George Cowie had done well at right back and both Craig Levein and Neil Berry were conspicuous players.

Unfortunately, Levein had been nursing a strain and had to withdraw from the Scotland team to play Holland in Eindhoven on April 29 in what seemed a pointless, pre-World Cup fixture with hardly any Anglos available.

John Robertson was in the pool, too, and Gary Mackay was called in as a last-minute replacement. Recognition for Hearts, at last, even if it was belated.

Offers were pouring in for the club to undertake tours. They had rejected an invitation to play in Iraq before the trip to Dundee and now there were calls from New Zealand, Jamaica and the Gambia. But foreign fields were not in the club's sights except the one at Dens Park!

HEARTS: Smith; Cowie, Whittaker; S. Jardine, Berry, Levein; Colquhoun, Black (I. Jardine), Clark, Mackay, Robertson.

CLYDEBANK: Gallacher; Dickson, Given; Maher, Auld, Treanor; Shanks, Hughes (Moore), Bain, Conroy, McCabe.

Referee — K. O'Donnell, Airdrie

PREMIER LEAGUE

Aberdeen	1	Rangers	1
Celtic	2	Dundee	0
Dundee United	1	St. Mirren	2
Hearts	1	Clydebank	0
Motherwell	3	Hibernian	1

	P	W	D	L	F	A	Pts
HEARTS	35	20	10	5	59	31	50
Celtic	34	18	10	6	60	38	46
Dundee United	35	17	11	7	57	30	45
Aberdeen	35	15	12	8	56	31	42
Rangers	35	12	9	14	51	45	33
Dundee	35	13	7	15	43	51	33
St. Mirren	35	13	5	17	42	58	31
Hibernian	35	11	6	18	48	61	28
Motherwell	34	7	6	21	33	62	20
Clydebank	35	6	8	21	29	71	20

May 3, 1986

Dundee 2, Hearts 0

This was to be the final carnival to mark the winning of the championship and more than 10,000 Hearts fans chanted and sang in praise of the team before and during the game.

One point from Dens Park was all Hearts needed to become Premier champions for the first time because Celtic could achieve no more than 50 points by beating St. Mirren at Paisley.

But the cheering fans were unaware of the drama behind the scenes as manager Alex MacDonald tried to patch up a team stricken by a sickness bug.

As the players trooped off the bus, Craig Levein was missing and that was the first hint of a problem. He was confined to bed, George Cowie was ill and several members of the team were less than well. Neil Berry had gone down on the Tuesday followed by Kenny Black, Brian Whittaker and John Colquhoun, all victims of this savage twist of fate. On the credit side, skipper Walter Kidd was back after suspension.

Aberdeen manager Alex Ferguson was a surprise visitor to watch Hearts before the Scottish Cup final and Dundee reaped the rewards from their biggest gate of the season.

Roddy McDonald was drafted into the defence and looked very much at ease against a Dundee attack that carried no threat in the first half. In fact, Roddy had a good header at the other end from a Gary Mackay corner, the ball going past the goalkeeper's right-hand upright.

There was a buzz around the ground as news came through of a goal burst by Celtic who were in a position to snatch the championship if Hearts lost.

Black replaced the struggling Whittaker at the start of the second half and Hearts began to create difficulties for themselves by leaving passes short.

Berry battled sternly in midfield where Ian Jardine, who had back trouble, and Mackay were not at their best. However, Henry Smith was not under pressure until he was hurt diving on a cross by Connor. Then, he pushed aside a fine effort by Mennie following the substitution of Kidd for McKinlay.

Colquhoun and John Robertson might have engineered a goal in two brisk breakaways but Dundee covered quickly and showed their willingness to go for a win by introducing McCormack for Smith.

Roddy McDonald goes hunting for a goal at Dundee but he is out of range of this first half centre

Hearts were under the whip but the minutes were ticking away and they still had the point in their grasp.

Until 73 minutes had gone when the roof fell in on Hearts. Brown flicked on a corner from Connor on the right and Albert Kidd was left unmarked to clip a right-foot shot past Smith from close in. It was the first time in the entire season that Hearts had lost a goal from a corner. Hearts were shattered and didn't have the strength or energy to hit back. The fans rallied behind them not appreciating the tiredness in the team and Kidd swooped to strike again with two minutes left to register his only League goals of the season.

Fans poured onto the pitch only to be turned back immediately by the police, and there was a bigger invasion at the finish as players laboured to reach the dressing rooms.

It was an agonising way to lose the title to Celtic on goal difference and, as hundreds of supporters gathered at the mouth of the tunnel hoping vainly for the team to reappear, the whole scene was an action replay of 1965.

Hundreds of fans gather around the tunnel at Dens Park, chanting for the players to come out. But the team members were much too dismayed to acknowledge the fans

In that season, Hearts had scored 90 goals but surrendered the League to Kilmarnock who won 2–0 at Tynecastle in the last game to become champions on goal average.

Hearts asked the Scottish League to switch to goal difference to encourage attacking play and the motion was accepted immediately.

This time Hearts would have been champions on the old goal average system of dividing the goals for by the goals against!

In retrospect, however, Dens Park was not the ideal place to try to clinch the championship, for Hearts had beaten Dundee only twice in three seasons in League matches. A jinx team for sure.

A scene from Dens Park that says it all. This unknown fan, sad and stunned, buries his head in his arms, still wondering how the championship had been ripped out of Hearts' grasp in those final minutes.

DUNDEE: Geddes; Shannon, McKinlay (Kidd); Glennie, Smith (McCormack), Duffy; Mennie, Brown, Harvey, Connor, Hendry.

HEARTS: Smith; Kidd, Whittaker (Black); S. Jardine, Berry, McDonald; Colquhoun, I. Jardine (W. McKay), Clark, G. Mackay, Robertson.

Referee – W. Crombie, Edinburgh.

Booking – McDonald.

PREMIER LEAGUE

Clydebank	0	Aberdeen	6
Dundee	2	Hearts	0
Hibernian	1	Dundee United	2
Rangers	2	Motherwell	0
St. Mirren	0	Celtic	5

	P	W	D	L	F	A	Pts
Celtic	36	20	10	6	67	38	50
HEARTS	36	20	10	6	59	33	50
Dundee United	36	18	11	7	59	31	47
Aberdeen	36	16	12	8	62	31	44
Rangers	36	13	9	14	53	45	35
Dundee	36	14	7	15	45	51	35
St. Mirren	36	13	5	18	42	63	31
Hibernian	36	11	6	19	49	63	28
Motherwell	36	7	6	23	33	66	20
Clydebank	36	6	8	22	29	77	20

Played Apr. 30 — Motherwell 0, Celtic 2

Hearts were the only team in the Premier League to have an unbeaten home record in the championship. They won five more points on their own ground than any of their rivals and conceded 10 goals in 18 games.

But Celtic regained those five points in away matches in which they scored 40 goals — 13 more than they had done at Parkhead.

Here is the tell-tale home and away table:

HOME AND AWAY TABLE

		Home Goals					Away Goals					
	P	W	D	L	F	A	W	D	L	F	A	Pts
Celtic	36	10	6	2	27	15	10	4	4	40	23	50
HEARTS	36	13	5	0	38	10	7	5	6	21	23	50
Dundee Utd	36	10	6	2	38	15	8	5	5	21	16	47
Aberdeen	36	11	4	3	38	15	5	8	5	24	16	44
Rangers	36	10	4	4	34	18	3	5	10	19	27	35
Dundee	36	11	2	5	32	20	3	5	10	13	31	35
St. Mirren	36	9	2	7	26	24	4	3	11	16	39	31
Hibernian	36	6	4	8	27	25	5	2	11	22	38	28
Motherwell	36	7	3	8	23	23	0	3	15	10	43	20
Clydebank	36	4	6	8	18	32	2	2	14	11	45	20

It is an interesting exercise to see how Hearts collected their 50 points, easily a club record considering that their previous best total was 36.

Dundee alone managed to break even in the four games but there is some satisfaction in the fact that five points were gained from Celtic — one of three teams who did not register a win against Hearts.

Hearts fared best against Hibernian in the derby matches which yielded seven points but there were no maximum eight-pointers despite the successful season.

This was the breakdown:

HOW POINTS WERE WON

	P	W	D	L	F	A	Pts
Hibernian	4	3	1	0	7	3	7
Motherwell	4	3	0	1	9	3	6
Rangers	4	3	0	1	9	4	6
Dundee United	4	2	2	0	7	2	6
St. Mirren	4	3	0	1	9	6	6
Clydebank	4	2	1	1	6	3	5
Celtic	4	1	3	0	4	3	5
Aberdeen	4	2	1	1	3	4	5
Dundee	4	1	2	1	5	5	4

The Scottish Cup

January 25, 1986

Third round at Tynecastle

Hearts 3, Rangers 2

There was only one Scottish Cup tie that caught the imagination of the football public at the start of the 17-week-long march to Hampden. It had to be all ticket and the 27,500 capacity crowd saw a tie to remember on a flinty surface.

A dramatic late winner for Hearts; a player sent off; and two more forced to retire in the first half following a nasty clash of heads. This was cup-tie fare at its entertaining best.

It was bound to be physical because both teams feared an instant exit from the competition and a drastic shortfall in earnings.

Kenny Black took an early knock and Henry Smith had attention after Bobby Williamson, previously warned for a push on Craig Levein, charged into him rather recklessly.

Tackles were quick and hard so that neither side had the opportunity to dictate and Craig Paterson was handling all Hearts' aerial attacks with ease.

But the tie lasted only 31 minutes for Paterson and Sandy Clark. They jumped for a ball yards outside the penalty area and banged their heads together.

A stretcher was called for Paterson, though he actually wanted to walk off, and Clark left holding a pad on a gash above his nose. Both players required stitches and the two managers, Alex MacDonald and Jock Wallace, were on the park re-arranging their forces.

Colin McAdam stepped into the spearhead role for Hearts whereas Rangers switched Dave McPherson into defence and introduced Bobby Russell into the midfield. Rangers' defence never looked the same again yet the Ibrox men swooped into the lead two minutes from half time.

Davie Cooper burst onto the scene for the first time, whipped over a superb centre and Ally McCoist flicked a glancing header into the net.

Hearts were not entitled to be behind but this was a sudden death affair with no second chances and they met the challenge.

In 49 minutes, Hearts were level through McAdam's first goal for the club. Full back Miller blocked efforts from Neil Berry and John Robertson on the goal-line and then the big substitute hammered the ball in from a few yards.

81

Sandy Clark hits a left-foot shot over the bar shortly before he and Craig Paterson had to quit after an accidental clash of heads in this Scottish Cup tie at Tynecastle

Burns scooped another net-bound try from McAdam off the line and Rangers were in trouble. With 55 minutes on the clock, it was 2-1 for Hearts as Gary Mackay, at the far post, pushed home a right-wing corner from John Colquhoun.

Neil Berry could have killed off Rangers when he dashed through with goalkeeper Walker to beat and mishit the ball wide of the goal. Was it to prove a costly miss?

Battling Rangers did their best work going forward and they equalised in 69 minutes. Smith and Levein couldn't decide who should clear a bouncing ball and Ian Durrant nipped in to beat them with a header.

Still, there were more thrills to come. Youth cap Derek Ferguson was ordered off for retaliation against Mackay and Rangers' obvious aim was to hang on for a replay.

They failed by five minutes, for John Robertson snatched the most opportunist winner when the ball broke loose from a duel between Walker and Berry. Tough, perhaps, on Rangers but a great game for Hearts fans!

Ian Jardine uses his head to keep Hearts in possession against Rangers in the Scottish Cup tie

HEARTS: Smith; Kidd, Black; S. Jardine, Levein, Berry; Colquhoun, I. Jardine, Clark (McAdam), Mackay, Robertson.

RANGERS: Walker; Burns, Miller; Dawson, Paterson (Russell), Durrant; McCoist, D. Ferguson, Williamson, McPherson, Cooper.

Referee – T. Muirhead, Stenhousemuir.

March 3, 1986

Fourth round at Douglas Park

Hamilton 1, Hearts 2

They should have struck a medal for goalkeeper Henry Smith who kept Hearts in the competition in an amazing finish on a frosted, heavily sanded pitch which had been deemed unplayable four times.

Henry was cheered off the field by grateful supporters as Hearts clung to their precarious lead in a fascinating finish on a chill Monday night.

When Gary Mackay scored Hearts' second goal in 66 minutes, it seemed the end of the road for Hamilton's plucky part-timers but they simply refused to accept defeat and somehow found reserves of energy to roast the Tynecastle defence.

Hamilton made five chances in their closing assault. Smith saved magnificently from McNaught and Brogan and three other fairly simple openings were scorned by Clarke, Jamieson and Brogan.

It was a terrific climax and nobody would have grudged the best team in the First Division another game for their fine performance on a treacherous ground.

Referee McGinlay had to delay the kick-off for 15 minutes to allow spectators into the ground, many of them forced to walk along the track to a position behind the goal because of the congestion in the covered enclosure.

However, the start was sensational. The powerful McNaught took a backheeled pass from Reid near the halfway line and raced up the right wing. His low centre was perfect and Brogan stroked the ball into the net for a goal that rocked Hearts in just 15 seconds!

But Hamilton were given no opportunity to dwell on their lead and Hearts were all square in three minutes. John Robertson rifled home a shot once Sandy Clark and Brian Whittaker had done the spadework.

Hearts went on to do most of the attacking in the half though there was an uneasiness about both defences in the conditions.

McNaught was immense in the Hamilton mid-line with his driving runs and he showed courage, too, in shrugging off a sore knock to stay on the park.

Hearts might have gone ahead several times before Hamilton's big finish but it was left to Gary Mackay to beat Ferguson with a perfectly placed shot from a pass by John Robertson.

Ferguson, though overshadowed subsequently by the man in the other goal, had an excellent save from a header by John Colquhoun before Robbo was replaced by Andy Watson with 14 minutes to go.

John was unhappy to be taken off and made his feelings clear by running straight up the tunnel. Manager MacDonald felt a change in tactics was required especially as Ian Jardine had been unable to play owing to a ligament injury which had been kept secret, and the team survived in a nail-biting finale.

HAMILTON: Ferguson; Sinclair, Hamill; McNaught, Jamieson, Mitchell; Sprott (Clarke), Pelosi, Reid, O'Neil (Phillips), Brogan.

HEARTS: Smith; Kidd, Black; S. Jardine, Berry, Levein; Colquhoun, Whittaker, Clark, Mackay, Robertson (Watson).

Referee – B. R. McGinlay, Balfron.

March 9, 1986

Quarter final at Tynecastle

Hearts 4, St. Mirren 1

This game was played on a Sunday to avoid a clash with the Hibs-Celtic tie at Easter Road and it attracted a 20,000 crowd.

Manager Alex MacDonald was pleased with the result, of course, though not with the display. But it may have been the early injury to Campbell Money, the St. Mirren goalkeeper, that took the edge off their play.

After three minutes, Money was concussed in a collision with Sandy Clark and there was a seven-minute delay while he received treatment. A somewhat groggy goalkeeper resumed his place temporarily, for he was led away when John Colquhoun shot home a pass from Gary Mackay two minutes later.

Subsequently, Money had a checkup in hospital and was allowed home that evening but his departure put Saints in a dilemma.

They had no recognised deputy and defender Neil Cooper reluctantly went into goal with Winnie pulled off the bench.

Easy range for John Colquhoun to shoot his first Scottish Cup goal for Hearts in the Sunday tie with St. Mirren

So Hearts were a goal ahead and facing a rookie goalkeeper. Surely, they couldn't fail to score a few goals.

Number two arrived in the first-half injury time as John Robertson headed in a free kick from Kenny Black. And within six minutes of the second half, Hearts were four in front.

Black beat Cooper with an 18 yards free kick and Robbo sank a penalty following a trip on Colquhoun.

St. Mirren went through the motions for the remainder of the match and it was to their credit that McGarvey pulled back a goal in 61 minutes. The ex-Scotland and Celtic centre forward had played well against crushing odds.

Colquhoun took a minor knock and Sandy Jardine quit prematurely to ease the pressure on a leg strain.

HEARTS: Smith; Kidd, Whittaker; S. Jardine (McDonald), Berry, Levein; Colquhoun (McKay), Black, Clark, Mackay, Robertson.

ST. MIRREN: Money (Winnie); Wilson, Abercromby (Rooney); Cooper, Godfrey, Clarke; Fitzpatrick, Mackie, McGarvey, Gallacher, Speirs.

Referee – R. B. Valentine, Dundee. Attendance – 20,655

Bookings – Whittaker, Colquhoun.

April 6, 1986

Semi final at Hampden Park

Dundee United 0, Hearts 1

Hearts set up camp at the Hospitality Inn at Irvine two days before the semi final to give the players privacy and let them concentrate on the game.

Although Ian Jardine played in a midweek reserve match against Hibs to confirm his fitness, manager Alex MacDonald maintained his policy of sticking with a successful team so Ian was on the bench.

Perhaps the most anxious member of the side was skipper Walter Kidd who was desperate for the match to be settled in 90 minutes. He was due to start a three-match ban on the following Tuesday and would miss any replay. He needn't have worried since 20,000 travelling fans roared Hearts into their first final for 10 years.

United had a couple of unexpected changes which gave the impression that their tactics amounted to a holding job. The lively winger, Kevin Gallacher, was left out until half time when Dundee trailed by a goal and a rethink was necessary.

Kenny Black and Billy Kirkwood were warned in the first couple of minutes for over-zealous tackles and that was an early pointer that the referee wanted no nonsense.

In fact, Gary Mackay was cautioned in only 10 minutes for a challenge on Redford after Bannon had floated a superb crossfield pass into the path of Kirkwood who lost control of the ball.

D

John Colquhoun is about to volley the goal which sent Hearts into the Scottish Cup Final and Dundee United to the sidelines at Hampden

Slack work by Henry Smith and Craig Levein suggested Hearts were too nervous to do themselves justice but one spectacular effort acted like a tranquilliser on the entire side.

Levein, out on the right touchline beside the South Stand, pitched a lob into the goalmouth. Paul Hegarty and Sandy Clark went up together and the ball came out to John Colquhoun, whose so-sweet right-foot volley was timed to perfection.

Thomson dived gallantly to his right but he hadn't an earthly and little John had snatched a goal out of nothing – yet one fit to win a semi final.

A deft pass from Brian Whittaker gave captain Kidd the chance to slam in a quick second goal. Walter's low right footer beat Thomson only to sweep past the right-hand post, fractionally out of range for the lunging Sandy Clark.

Colquhoun's forceful runs worried the Tannadice defence, just as a diving header from Gough was deflected for a corner in a moment of anxiety at the other end.

Still, it had been an easy half for goalkeeper Smith who was to earn his bonus in the second period. A snappy head flick from Sturrock allowed Redford to unleash a drive that Henry turned behind.

United were more menacing now and determined to put the total emphasis on attack. That plan almost came unstuck when Black fired a Mackay-made chance too high.

Smith pounced on a header from Redford and stopped a close-in try by Sturrock to deny United an equaliser. Those were vital saves as Hearts defended with typical dourness to the end.

John Colquhoun pipped Henry Smith for the man of the match award and five bookings meant a deduction of £1750 from the sponsorship money on offer. However, Hearts surrendered only £700 of their £3,500.

DUNDEE UNITED: Thomson; Malpas, Holt; Gough, Hegarty, Narey; Bannon (Beedie), Redford, Kirkwood (Gallacher), Sturrock, Dodds.

HEARTS: Smith; Kidd, Whittaker; S. Jardine, Berry, Levein; Colquhoun, Black, Clark, Mackay (I. Jardine), Robertson.

Referee – B. R. McGinlay, Balfron. Attendance – 30,872.

Bookings – Mackay, S. Jardine.

May 10, 1986

Final at Hampden Park

Hearts 0, Aberdeen 3

Hearts breezed into Hampden from their Seamill Hydro retreat to a rapturous pre-match welcome from some of the near 40,000 fans who were there to cheer them.

It had been a week of anxiety with injuries and illness and the club had contemplated closing the ground for a couple of days earlier in the week.

However, the sickness virus seemed to have gone with John Robertson and Ian Jardine the last victims. Ian, unfortunately, was counted out with a back injury and Colin McAdam was unfit, too.

But Walter Kidd had recovered from a burst blood vessel in his foot and the players were in good heart after the disappointment of losing the championship a week earlier.

All was not well in the Aberdeen camp, for star forward Eric Black had been excluded from the pool earlier in the week after conducting a private transfer deal with the French club, Metz, while the powerful Neil Simpson was injured.

The grey-shirted Hearts (they had lost the toss to wear their normal colours) began confidently on a windy afternoon of sunshine and showers.

But, in less than five minutes, they allowed Aberdeen to snatch the all-important first goal. Hewitt gathered a long clearance from Miller and had no challengers as he turned towards goal.

The Tynecastle defenders backtracked to their cost and only tried to close in on Hewitt as he struck a low, well-placed left-foot shot past Henry Smith from the edge of the box.

It was a bad goal to lose so early though Hearts galloped back into the game with haste. In the course of the first half, Smith saved superbly from Hewitt who hit a beauty from 35 yards and also McDougall whose glancing header spelled danger.

Yet one wonders how the fortunes might have changed if Hearts had taken two glorious chances.

John Robertson seized on a header from Gary Mackay to loft the ball gently over Jim Leighton's head after the Aberdeen defence had poured out of the goalmouth.

It looked like the equaliser but, to Robertson's agony, the ball dropped just over the bar ...

Near the break, the tireless Neil Berry worked his way down the right and flashed a centre towards the far post where Mackay met the ball left-footed to send it two feet wide of the far post.

It was felt, generally, that Hearts were unlucky to be behind but they needed a quickie in the second half to bounce back.

Sadly, Aberdeen's timing was similar to the first half and Hewitt supplied their second goal in 49 minutes.

The Dons were delighted with the move in which McDougall dummied a low centre from Weir to allow Hewitt to sidefoot the ball into the net. Hearts were concerned that they had not been more attentive.

Hearts refused to accept defeat and had one last throw to save the game. Walter Kidd might have had a penalty when he went down in the box; Leighton saved smartly from Robertson; and Barry blasted

Hearts had their chances to get back onto level terms in the first half of the Scottish Cup final and Gary Mackay was only inches wide with this left-foot shot as a relieved Willie Miller looked on

a right footer against the crossbar. When that shot stayed out, the players knew it wasn't to be.

Substitute Billy Stark, who had replaced the injured McMaster, headed home a Weir cross in 75 minutes and, subsequently, scored another which was disallowed.

But Hearts' punishment was not over. Skipper Kidd, booked in the first half, and then warned for a further foul on Hewitt, was sent off with 13 minutes left after throwing the ball at an opponent while Mackay was being cautioned.

Frustration, dejection—call it what you will. Walter made the long, lonely walk to the dressing room with head bowed. Suspended at the start of next season along with Mackay who had reached the penalty points limit.

Hearts were beaten and their self discipline had slipped but thousands of flag-waving fans kept up their chants even after the final whistle.

Hearts keeper Henry Smith thwarts an Aberdeen attack at Hampden

Tearful players dragged their legs to the Mount Florida end to salute the punters who had provided such marvellous encouragement during the season. Hundreds stayed behind outside the stand to cheer their heroes onto the bus.

In victory, Hearts would have gone to the Norton House Hotel on the outskirts of Edinburgh and switched into the open-topped double decker for the parade through the city.

Alas, it was another occasion on which Edinburgh had been denied a night of celebration. One Scottish Cup triumph in 80 years seemed a scant return from Lady Luck who had played two fiendish tricks on Hearts in the space of eight days, robbing them of an honour richly deserved.

But it had been an incredible season—perhaps just a sample of things to come.

HEARTS: Smith; Kidd, Whittaker; S. Jardine, Berry, Levein; Colquhoun, Black, Clark, Mackay, Robertson.
Subs did not play—Cowie, W. McKay.

ABERDEEN: Leighton; McKimmie, McQueen; McMaster (Stark), McLeish, W. Miller; Hewitt (J. Miller), Cooper, McDougall, Bett, Weir.

Referee—H. Alexander, Irvine. Attendance—62,841

Bookings—Kidd, Berry, Mackay, Robertson.

Sent Off—Kidd.

Cup Final action . . .

Willie Miller left stranded by Sandy Clark

On-the-ball magic from John Robertson

A close encounter of the wrestling kind between Walter Kidd and Weir of Aberdeen

An almighty scramble in the Aberdeen goalmouth

John Robertson looks on as Colquhoun slips past Miller

The fans show their gratitude to the team for the wonderful entertainment they have provided over the season

The Skol League Cup

August 20, 1985

Montrose 1, Hearts 3

Having lost 6-2 the previous Saturday to St Mirren at Love Street in the League, Hearts began their Skol League Cup campaign at Links Park, Montrose in need of a boost to morale.

On what was an appalling August night of heavy and persistent rain, Hearts had brought back their captain Walter Kidd, leaving out young Jimmy Sandison, into defence. Craig Levein was pushed forward into midfield in a bid to tighten things up.

With the Links Park pitch resembling a leaky sponge, curious goals were always going to be the order of the night. Kidd, who was playing his first competitive match of the season after suspension, duly obliged with a very odd effort indeed.

John Colquhoun had started the move and Kidd made space down the right before hitting a loping 30 yards cross. Sandy Clark failed to make contact with the ball in the box which nonetheless skidded into the net at the backpost.

A goal up after 24 minutes, Hearts should have been in easy street. But the Tynecastle side's commanding winter form was still a couple of months away. And Montrose equalised just before half time through John Sheran.

Hearts got back into the groove after the interval when John Robertson restored their lead, steering the ball into the corner of the net after good work by Sandy Clark.

It was plain sailing thereafter with John Colquhoun perhaps just a shade fortunate to get the credit for Hearts' third goal which took a deflection off Cusiter on its way past the Montrose goalkeeper.

If Sandy Clark's industry was the outstanding feature of the second-round tie from Hearts' angle, the most worrying aspect of the game was a knock to Levein, who had to be taken off with a leg injury before the end.

MONTROSE: Charles; Barr, McClelland; Cusiter, Sheran, Forbes; Allan, Bennett, Somner, Lennox, Millar. Subs – Caithness, Wright.

HEARTS: Smith; Kidd, Whittaker; Jardine, R. MacDonald, Levein; Colquhoun, Watson, Clark, Robertson, Mackay. Subs – Sandison, McNaughton.

Referee – A. Roy (Aberdeen).

Booking – Whittaker.

August 27, 1985

Hearts 2, Stirling Albion 1 (after extra time)

Craig Levein's injury turned out not to be as serious as was first feared and the Under-21 internationalist was in his usual place the following week against Stirling Albion at Tynecastle. He was hardly 100 per cent fit, however, as a 'flu virus had spread through Hearts' first-team squad.

Sandy Jardine, John Colquhoun and Brian Whittaker were the other individuals affected as Hearts suffered an August evening of high anxiety against Second Division opponents who belied their part-time status.

McGulley, a veteran of the lower divisions, had caused Hearts numerous problems in the first half with a series of darting runs. It was entirely justified on the run-of-play that the visitors should take the lead a couple of minutes before the interval.

It was a fine effort, stemming from a McGulley corner which was finished off by a thrilling left-foot volley from Scott Maxwell. At that point Hearts must have wondered if they'd made a wise move two years previously in freeing the player.

Hearts made a change after the interval when Sandy Jardine stayed in the dressing-room with a knock and Paul Cherry came into the attack. There was plenty of pressure and eventually an equaliser was headed home by Brian McNaughton in the 75th minute after good work by Robertson.

The tie spilled over into extra time when Robertson was again the provider with a cross that substitute Cherry headed past the Stirling goalkeeper in the 101st minute.

By that point Hearts knew they were into an attractive quarter-final tie against Aberdeen at Pittodrie, but on the form shown against Stirling it was less obvious how they were going to make further progress in the competition.

HEARTS: Smith; Cowie, Whittaker; Jardine, MacDonald, Levein; Colquhoun, Watson, McNaughton, Robertson, Black. Subs – Sandison, Cherry.

STIRLING ALBION: Graham; Dawson, Spence; Aitchison, McTeague, Maxwell; Hoggan, Walker, Irvine, Grant, McGulley. Subs – Thomson, Ormond.

Referee – J. Duncan (Gorebridge).

September 4, 1985

Aberdeen 1, Hearts 0

Walter Kidd and Sandy Clark, who had missed the Stirling tie because of suspension, were back in harness for the trip to Aberdeen. However their presence hardly seemed to lift a Hearts' side who had great difficulty in building up any kind of steam in the quarter final.

John Colquhoun had been left out of Hearts' starting line-up and it soon became clear that the Edinburgh side were more interested in containment than taking the match to Aberdeen.

True, Kenny Black almost deceived Leighton early on in the game with a long-range effort following a clever pass from Gary Mackay.

But for the most part Aberdeen dominated without having to sparkle on what was an undeniably flat occasion. Full back Stuart McKimmie caused Hearts problems with his forward runs and it was from his cross in the 24th minute that the tie was decided.

Goalkeeper Henry Smith and centre half Roddy MacDonald got themselves in a tangle at this one. Smith had failed to grasp the cross cleanly and MacDonald booted the ball clear – only to look on in horror as the rebound from Eric Black's body crossed the line.

The story of the second half was one of steady Aberdeen pressure. They didn't have to do anything special to keep control of the game and would have won more comfortably but for a series of first-rate saves by Henry Smith, who made amends for his first-half slip.

John Colquhoun was pushed on for John Robertson in the last 30 minutes, but the substitution made little difference on a night when the Skol Cup's fireworks were all reserved for the tie at Easter Road where Hibs beat Celtic 4-3 on penalties following a 4-4 draw after extra time.

Aberdeen went on to beat Hibs 3-0 in the final at Hampden and Hearts at least had the consolation of going out to the best team in the competition.

ABERDEEN: Leighton; McKimmie, Mitchell; Stark, McLeish, Miller; Black, Simpson, McDougall, Bett, Weir. Subs – Cooper, Hewitt.

HEARTS: Smith; Kidd, Whittaker; Jardine, MacDonald, Levein; Watson, Mackay, Clark, Robertson, Black. Subs – Cherry, Colquhoun.

Referee – R. B. Valentine (Dundee).

Bookings – Levein, Whittaker, Robertson.

The Management Team

Manager – Alex MacDonald

As a midfield player with St Johnstone, Rangers and latterly Hearts, Alex MacDonald was easy to underestimate. His peerless ability to dispatch the first-time pass accurately didn't always get the recognition it deserved.

And as a manager the modest MacDonald, with little or no fanfare, turned Hearts around from a club that suffered from the yo-yo syndrome (constantly dividing their time between the Premier and First Divisions) into a side capable of making a healthy challenge for major honours.

The truth was that MacDonald enjoyed playing so much he hardly gave a thought to becoming a manager. Like his friend and assistant Sandy Jardine, MacDonald wanted to keep on playing throughout his thirties. But wear and tear on the calf muscles prevented him achieving that particular ambition in the first team.

MacDonald was with Rangers for 12 years before moving to Tynecastle in 1980. A year later, after the arrival of Wallace Mercer, he was made player-coach in succession to Tony Ford. It wasn't until 1982 that MacDonald was confirmed as manager, not because Hearts didn't want him, but in order to avoid putting pressure on him.

In spite of this apparent reluctance to take centre-stage, MacDonald has enjoyed being a manager, and is grateful that the club's directors understood it wouldn't be an overnight job to remould the team.

With the assistance of Jardine, coach Walter Borthwick and reserve coach John Binnie, MacDonald brought organisation, flair and commitment to Hearts' play.

He also worked wonders on the transfer market. Of the players on the Tynecastle books in February 1982, only Henry Smith, Walter Kidd, Sandy Jardine, Roddy McDonald, Gary Mackay and John Robertson remained in 1985/86.

Men like Brian Whittaker, Neil Berry, Iain Jardine, Kenny Black, John Colquhoun and Sandy Clark were all acquired from the cash provided by the sale of David Bowman to Coventry.

In Under-21 international players such as Levein, Robertson and Mackay, Hearts have more saleable assets than for many years. And in the management team of MacDonald and Jardine, Hearts have enjoyed the services of a pair who, in Wallace Mercer's words, helped get the club's act together.

As a young man Alex MacDonald was a cross-country runner. In the course of season 1985/86 he proved that as a team boss he's not lacking in staying power, and deservedly was acclaimed as manager of the year.

Alex MacDonald   Sandy Jardine

Assistant-manager – Sandy Jardine

Born, 31/12/48.
Signed, 1981.
Born, Edinburgh.
Number of Appearances – 43

It wasn't a bad year for the more mature type of player, what with Kenny Dalglish, the Liverpool player-manager, winning his one hundredth cap for Scotland and Sandy Jardine making his 1,000th senior appearance, fittingly for Hearts against his old club Rangers in the November of 1985.

Like Dalglish, Jardine always understood the importance of discipline and his strict training habits paid off handsomely in a career that actually touched new peaks in the player's 37th year.

The combination of Jardine and Craig Levein at the centre of Hearts' defence was a significant factor in the team's success. Both men were footballers first, stoppers second, and Hearts reaped the benefit of building intelligently from the back.

Even in his Rangers' days, Jardine was never an overly physical defender. Certainly he would have succeeded in playing on the Continent because the emphasis in his approach was always on subtlety rather than strength. As Hearts chased both the championship and the Scottish Cup, it was Jardine's coolness and consistency which did much to maintain their long unbeaten run.

Even at a time when his ambitions inclined more and more to the managerial side of things, nonetheless Sandy Jardine was able to contribute an enormous amount on the field.

Modestly he put his own efforts down to the help of others, stating that it wasn't difficult for an older player such as himself to look impressive when the rest of the side were acquitting themselves so well. Scottish Brewers obviously thought differently when they made Jardine one of their players of the month and he was the choice of the Scottish Football Writers' Association as player of the year – the first Hearts' player to be honoured in this way.

First-team coach – Walter Borthwick

While most of the managerial limelight falls on Alex MacDonald and Sandy Jardine, first-team coach Walter Borthwick is a highly respected figure at Tynecastle. He was a player himself with spells at St Mirren and Dunfermline, where he also did some coaching.

Having subsequently carved out a successful career for himself in the civil service, Borthwick was nonetheless keen to return to a job in football. When Hearts offered him the chance of a behind-the-scenes position he jumped at it.

Borthwick gave himself a couple of years to see if the gamble was worthwhile – and by 1986 Hearts were riding high. Alex MacDonald was always quick to pay tribute to Borthwick as an important part of the backroom team responsible for the turn around in Hearts' fortunes.

Second-team coach – John Binnie

An accountant outwith football, John Binnie's involvement with Hearts as second-team coach was on a part-time basis. He was a former Hearts' player who was delighted to come back to Tynecastle to help out with the promising youngsters in the second team. His advice and enthusiasm were sources of great encouragement to the younger members of the staff.

The Players

Henry Smith

Born, 10/3/56
Signed, 1981
Place of Birth, Lanark
Number of Appearances – 44

A new broom was in business at Tynecastle in 1981 with sweeping changes at board level as well as on the playing side. Willie Pettigrew and Derek Addison from Dundee United were the big money buys while other new faces like Pat Byrne, Roddy MacDonald, Stewart Maclaren, Gerry McCoy, Peter Marinello and Derek Strickland all got their fair share of newspaper coverage.

The arrival of goalkeeper Henry Smith from Leeds United went almost

Henry Smith

104

unnoticed amidst the hubbub that saw Hearts attempt to make a fresh start by splashing out over £300,000 on the transfer market.

However the tall, well-built 30-year-old possibly turned out to be as significant a signing as any Hearts made in that year of upheaval. While his predecessor, John Brough, had done well in the First Division, Smith soon established himself as a favourite with the Tynecastle faithful.

Chants of 'Henry, Henry' would greet the goalkeeper's more spectacular performances. If, at first, Smith was prone to blow hot and cold – it seemed he was either unbeatable or giving away soft goals – by season 1985/86 the goalkeeper had attained a new level of maturity and consistency.

Next to internationalists Jim Leighton and Alan Rough, Smith was the Premier Division's most able goalkeeper. On the odd occasion when the side's form was below par, as it was against Hamilton at Douglas Park in the Scottish Cup tie, Smith could be relied on to save the day. His work at cross-balls was much improved on previous seasons while his instinctive athleticism in dealing with direct shots at goal remained impressive.

Walter Kidd

Born, 10/3/58
Signed, 1977
Place of birth, Edinburgh
Number of Appearances – 35

Hearts' captain and the longest-serving player at Tynecastle in many ways typified the spirit of the entire squad. An honest, wholehearted character with bags of enthusiasm, Kidd produced his best form since joining the club in 1977 from Newtongrange Star.

Brought to Hearts by the late Willie Ormond, Kidd was an adaptable type who figured in a number of different roles (he was always, for instance, an effective marker in the midfield area against Gordon Strachan when the little Scotland player was at Pittodrie) before settling down as a right-back.

It was announced during the season that a testimonial committee, to be chaired by the former Hearts centre-forward Donald Ford, was to be formed and that the 28-year-old Kidd would become only the fifth Hearts player to be honoured in this way.

Wallace Mercer, the club chairman, pointed out that loyalty didn't have to be financially crippling for players and used Kidd as an example to the

Craig Levein and John Robertson congratulate skipper Walter Kidd on being awarded a testimonial year as the clubs' longest serving player

younger element of the benefits that could be earned by staying with the club.

In a playing sense, after so much experience of the lean years in the First Division and the constant battles to either avoid relegation or win promotion, Kidd seemed to relish the chase for the title. He was capable of making brisk runs forward in support of the attack while keeping things simple at the back.

Brian Whittaker

Born, 23/9/56
Signed, 1984
Place of Birth, Glasgow
Number of Appearances – 31

The former Partick Thistle and Celtic man had tasted disappointment in football before his transfer to Tynecastle, not least in having a six-figure

Brian Whittaker

transfer fee put on his head when he was at Firhill. This high valuation prevented the defender making a possible move to West Germany.

The Bundesliga's loss eventually turned out to be Hearts' gain. After making around 20 first-team appearances for Celtic without establishing himself as an automatic choice, Whittaker was snapped up by Hearts for a bargain fee of £25,000 in the summer of 1984.

In fact Alex MacDonald had tried to sign Whittaker the year before, but Thistle had wanted £60,000 and so Hearts had to bide their time. The player was worth waiting for, because he complemented Hearts' policy of playing football out of defence.

When Ian Jardine was fit and involved in the midfield, Whittaker had competition from Kenny Black for the left-back spot and this rivalry undoubtedly helped to keep both players on their toes.

Whittaker always had a reputation as a stylish player with a tendency towards casualness. In the course of Hearts' long unbeaten run, however, there wasn't much sign of slackness on the defender's part. He said his ambition was to help the club put silverware back in the board-room again and his performances reflected that commitment.

Craig Levein

Born, 22/10/64
Signed, 1983
Place of Birth, Dunfermline
Number of Appearances – 41

Even as a teenager with Cowdenbeath, Craig Levein was being tipped as a future Scotland player. And when the elegant defender was selected by Alex Ferguson for the squad that travelled to Israel in January he duly became the first Hearts player to be included in a full international pool since Jim Cruickshank had kept goal against Romania in 1975.

Levein, who had already won Under-21 honours, didn't make it into the World Cup squad for Mexico because of the presence of seasoned international centre-backs like Willie Miller, Alex McLeish, David Narey and Alan Hansen.

Certainly, as Ferguson acknowledged, Levein had been a genuine contender on the strength of his club form. 'He's an outstanding athlete with good stamina, speed and ability', commented the Scotland manager.

But with others ahead of him in the representative queue, Levein was able to concentrate on the domestic front. He won both young player and player of the month awards in recognition of his defensive excellence.

Together with Sandy Jardine, who drilled his young colleague in good habits, Levein changed the way Hearts played. Without an orthodox stopper centre-half there was an emphasis on football out of defence which made a huge contribution to the team's lengthy unbeaten run.

Levein had originally been used by Hearts as a midfield player and his experience of playing in that area brought a quick, positive approach to his work at the back.

Neil Berry

Born, 6/4/63
Signed, 1984
Place of Birth, Edinburgh
Number of Appearances – 37

It didn't make headlines at the time, but Hearts' signing of Neil Berry from Bolton just before Christmas in 1984 had to go down as one of the shrewdest moves made by Alex MacDonald and Sandy Jardine.

Craig Levein

Neil Berry

Although his promise had been evident as a Scottish youth inter-nationalist, Berry, who was a Hearts' supporter, hadn't settled all that well at Bolton where he only played eight first-team games.

Apart from homesickness for Edinburgh, Berry didn't make a great impact as a centre-half with the English club. It was to Hearts' credit that they spotted other qualities in the player and set about honing Berry's talents as the natural replacement for Dave Bowman.

In fact Berry brought a more streamlined aggression to Hearts' midfield. Aberdeen's Chris Anderson rated him the best new player seen in Scotland during the season and it wasn't long before wealthy English clubs were eyeing a talent that Hearts had scooped for nothing.

It was particularly impressive that while Berry produced the drive behind Hearts' play, he wasn't in any way an overly physical player and was very rarely booked.

His contribution to Hearts' play wasn't just a negative one, though there was no doubt he was the type of player who was hard to play against. Berry's quickness and strong running more often than not caused problems for opposition defences.

Kenny Black

Born, 29/11/63
Signed, 1984
Place of Birth, Stenhousemuir
Number of Appearances – 30 (6)

It was joked around Tynecastle when Kenny Black joined the club from Motherwell that at least he could rely on the calming influence of Willie Johnston to help him settle in.

Black moved to Edinburgh in the close-season of 1984 with something of a reputation for physical play, which stemmed from his early days at Ibrox. In his first two games with Rangers, Black was booked twice and sent off once. He looked a player with a short fuse.

However Alex MacDonald and Sandy Jardine were confident that the versatile 22-year-old who was capable of operating either in midfield or defence, had calmed down since his Rangers' days.

Their faith was justified and Black, who was purchased for a miserly £30,000, was one of Hearts' most disciplined as well as effective players in 1985–86.

No doubt Hearts' success story encouraged the player to improve his disciplinary record for there was no guarantee once a player had dropped out of the side, either because of suspension or injury, that he would automatically win his place back.

There were many who thought Hearts played their best football of the season in a creative sense when Black was at left back and Ian Jardine was in the midfield. However the left-sided player was seen more often in a midfield role where his contributions were most noticeable at set-pieces. At free-kicks and corner-kicks he impressed as the best striker of a dead ball on the staff.

Kenny Black   Gary Mackay

Gary Mackay

Born, 23/1/64
Signed, 1980
Place of Birth, Edinburgh
Number of Appearances – 37 (2)

The Under-21 internationalist was one of a number of Hearts players to be honoured during the course of the season, winning the Fine Fare young footballer of the month award for January. Mackay's notable form during that month took him to within a whisker of being selected for the Scotland squad that travelled to play Israel in Tel Aviv.

There were many who held the opinion that Mackay was one of the key reasons why Hearts flourished in 1986. Having made his first-team debut as long ago as 1980 at the tender age of 16, Mackay combined youth and experience in the one package. In common with John Robertson and John Colquhoun he had the skill to turn a game Hearts' way.

Bobby Moncur had signed Mackay for Hearts and he used to tell the story of how, knowing that Manchester United were interested in the player, he had locked the door of the manager's room at Tynecastle until Mackay had pledged himself to the club.

Having caught the eye of late Scotland manager Jock Stein in season 1983-84 with a series of impressive performances (Mackay was always a favourite of Stein's) the midfield player was unfortunate to sustain an ankle injury in 1984 that hampered his progress the following year.

But the young publican was back to his best by the autumn of 1985 as Hearts embarked on their quest for the title. Mackay's shrewd use of the ball and ability to take on defenders was now matched to a greater physical strength which improved his overall contribution to the midfield.

Ian Jardine

Born, 17/2/55
Signed, 1985
Place of Birth, Irvine
Number of Appearances – 20 (5)

The former Kilmarnock and Partick Thistle player's hopes of making an impact in the Premier Division seemed to have all but disappeared when he moved to play football in Cyprus with Anorthosis, under the guidance of Peter Cormack.

But when Hearts heard that the 31-year-old midfield player wanted to come back to Scotland they stepped in before Dundee to secure his signature in June of 1985. As it turned out, an injury prevented Jardine from being involved with the first team until mid-September.

Perhaps it wasn't entirely coincidental that when he started a game for the first time against Dundee on October 5, Hearts gained a draw and went on to embark on a record unbeaten run of Premier Division fixtures.

Jardine brought variety to Hearts' midfield play with his longer passing style. He was also an individual who packed a ferocious shot and was able to contribute a few goals.

For long enough he didn't know what it was to start and finish a match on the losing side for Hearts and there was a valid school of thought that argued the team's best performances often coincided with the inclusion of the Ayrshire player.

On the ball with Ian Jardine

It was a happy Easter for John Colquhoun, who received an Easter egg as part of his prize for being named as Scottish Brewers player of the month for February. The £250 cheque and firkin of ale stayed with John. The Easter egg was presented to the Royal Hospital for Sick Children

John Colquhoun

Born, 14/7/63
Signed, 1985
Place of Birth, Stirling
Number of Appearances – 43 (1)

The former Celtic and Stirling Albion man was another one of the ugly duckling players who turned into a swan at Tynecastle. In the course of 18 months at Parkhead, Colquhoun was regarded only as an understudy to Davie Provan and turned out a mere 14 times for Celtic in season 1984/85.

Hearts paid out £50,000 for Colquhoun but it was significant at the time of the player's transfer that Alex MacDonald refrained from describing his latest acquisition as a winger.

As also happened with Neil Berry, Hearts spotted that there was more to the player than first met the eye. In his time with Stirling, Colquhoun had been used through the middle. And in conjunction with Sandy Clark and John Robertson, he brought a more fluid approach to the Hearts' attack.

Like his colleagues up front, Colquhoun was a hard worker as well as an able individual. He had a talent for running at defenders and was one of those players who could pace his game so that he had a significant contribution to make in the closing phase of a match.

He was another individual to win the Scottish Brewers player of the month award and made headlines when he was introduced to the Labour party leader Neil Kinnock in Perth. Unlike most footballers who say they want to meet either Samantha Fox or the Pools man when they fill out their biographies for the club programme, Colquhoun, who has ambitions to be an MP when his playing days are over, wanted to meet Mr Kinnock.

Sandy Clark

Born, 28/10/56
Signed, 1984
Place of Birth, Airdrie
Number of Appearances – 40

When it became clear that Hearts required a replacement for veteran striker Jimmy Bone, the club couldn't have got either a better influence in the dressing-room or a more able individual to lead the attack than Sandy Clark.

The 29-year-old centre forward cost West Ham and Rangers £300,000 in transfer fees before Hearts snapped him up for a bargain price. Ironically Clark went on to reproduce for Hearts his best form since he'd led the Airdrie attack as a part-timer.

Clark's battling qualities and strength in the air were important parts of Hearts' attacking system. In fact, Alex Miller, the St Mirren manager, once praised Clark's attitude after a game as typical of the spirit that pushed Hearts into the chase for the title.

In many ways the identikit Hearts goal in the course of the season involved a cross from Colquhoun, a knock-down from Clark and the finish from Robertson.

But Clark also delivered his own fair share of goals, showing a confidence in front of goal that had not been evident during his time at Ibrox. It was doubtful whether there was a more awkward Scottish centre forward than Clark to play against during the course of the year. His all-action style always ensured a hectic 90 minutes for the opposition centre half.

Sandy Clark

John Robertson

Born, 2/10/64
Signed, 1980
Place of Birth, Edinburgh
Number of Appearances – 42 (1)

In spite of his tender years, the 21-year-old striker had been around Tynecastle long enough to remember the lean times that had brought the club close to bankruptcy.

Signed from Edina Hibs in 1980 – apart from club captain Walter Kidd, Robertson and Gary Mackay were the longest-serving players on the club

John Robertson ... putting on the style

books – the slim forward had been connected with a big money move to Spurs in season 1984/85.

But Robertson, on an improved contract, opted to stay with the club he supported as well as played for. After the signing of John Colquhoun from Celtic, Robertson's role in the side changed yet the goals kept coming, even if the striker was more often to be found in the area between midfield and attack.

Perhaps Robertson's deftness of execution in front of goal, not to mention his natural footballing intelligence, didn't make quite as dramatic an impact as in the 1983 season when Hearts had just won promotion to the top ten of the Premier Division.

But if anything the statistics showed that as the club's top scorer Robertson had surpassed his previous achievements with Hearts. And in the latter part of the season he also solved the club's spot-kick dilemma which had seen Gary Mackay, John Colquhoun and Kenny Black all miss penalties.

Notwithstanding his goals, John Robertson's most significant contribution to Hearts' season was his ability to produce a touch of the unexpected when it mattered most. It was a talent shared by John Colquhoun and Gary Mackay – and one that played a key role in setting Hearts apart from the rest.

Colin McAdam

Born, 28/8/51
Signed, 1985
Place of Birth, Glasgow
Number of Appearances – 0 (6)

Like Ian Jardine, McAdam returned to Scottish football and a stint with Hearts after a short spell in Australia where he was inhibited by a rib injury. He grabbed the headlines in the 3-2 Scottish Cup win over Rangers, coming on as a substitute for the injured Sandy Clark to score

A cheerful smile from Colin McAdam in the boot room

against his old club. However it was his influence off the field as much as on it that was appreciated by the rest of the players.

After the departure of winger Willie Johnston, Hearts felt they needed an experienced, cheerful individual to help the younger players in the dressing-room. McAdam filled the bill ideally and was regularly involved in the run-in to the championship as a substitute.

Although Hearts signed him on a free transfer, Colin had cost Rangers more than £160,000 when a Tribunal fixed the price that Partick Thistle had to be paid in 1980.

Billy Mackay

Born, 27/10/60
Signed, 1986
Place of Birth, Glenrothes
Number of Appearances – 0 (4)

Signing on-time for Billy Mackay with Alex MacDonald and Sandy Jardine at his side

When the 25-year-old former Rangers winger signed for Hearts in February he must have felt like a man who had escaped the gallows. In his time at Ibrox, Mackay had sustained a serious knee injury which required the player to retire from the game in 1984.

But after being given a part-time scouting job by Hearts, Mackay underwent an examination by the club physiotherapist and subsequently undertook a series of leg-strengthening exercises. His recovery culminated in Mackay making his first-team debut as a substitute against Celtic at Parkhead. The Fifer was regarded by the management as a valuable addition to the first-team playing pool.

Rangers had given Billy a testimonial game when his playing days seemed to be over and the cash enabled him to become a publican in Coupar Angus.

Andy Watson

Born, 3/9/59
Signed, 1984
Place of birth, Aberdeen
Number of Appearances – 11 (5)

Hearts moved to sign the former Aberdeen player from Leeds United after completing the £200,000 transfer of David Bowman to Coventry City. He was a first-team regular until the arrival of Neil Berry and Ian Jardine quickened the competition for places in Hearts' midfield.

A forceful type of player who was normally at his best on heavier grounds, Watson wore the number eight jersey throughout August and September but thereafter figured mainly as a substitute. It was a role he was accustomed to from his days with the Pittodrie club.

Roddy MacDonald

Born, 30/8/54
Signed, 1981
Place of Birth, Dingwall
Number of Appearances – 13 (1)

The big centre-half was another first-team regular in August and September who had to be content with more occasional appearances once Hearts hit their unbeaten stride. A solid dependable defender with outstanding ability in the air, Hearts were fortunate to have such an experienced player on stand-by.

E

Andy Watson ... an
Aberdonian in the
midfield ranks

Roddy MacDonald

George Cowie ...
a handyman for
defensive areas

When Sandy Jardine missed a rare game against Motherwell in March the former Celtic man stepped back in as if he'd never been away, helping Hearts to keep a clean sheet and scoring at the other end. It was to Hearts' credit that they were able to involve players like MacDonald and Watson in the drive for honours even though they were usually on the fringes of the team.

As in his days with Celtic, the former Highland League player can be at his most useful in dead-ball situations, using his head to score goals rather than stop them.

George Cowie

Born, 6/5/61
Signed, 1983
Place of Birth, Buckie
Number of Appearances – 9

The former West Ham player gave Hearts experienced cover in the full-back positions, and was usually drafted into the side when captain Walter Kidd wasn't available.

The 24-year-old Highlander who had moved to Tynecastle after a spell with West Ham was more often seen in the first team before the signing of

Brian Whittaker. An honest, wholehearted type of defender, Cowie could always be relied on to make his presence felt in a game.

He has not been the luckiest player since arriving at Tynecastle and injuries prevented him from playing a more substantial role in the past season.

Paul
Cherry

Paul Cherry

Born, 14/10/64
Signed, 1983
Place of birth, Derby
Number of Appearances – 3 (4)

The versatile 21-year-old could fit in either up front or in defence. He made a handful of appearances early on in the season and figured in the significant 2-0 win over Dundee United at Tynecastle in September.

Cherry scored his first goal in the senior team against Stirling Albion in the Skol Cup and when he wasn't playing for the reserves he was a handy golfer in his spare time.

Brian McNaughton ... a
nippy centre forward with
an eye for goal

Jimmy
Sandison

Brian McNaughton

Born, 22/1/63
Signed, 1984
Place of birth, Edinburgh
Number of Appearances – 3 (2)

The former Post Office worker who only turned full-time at the start of 1985/86 was out of action with a broken collar-bone for a spell. A slim, fair-haired striker in the John Robertson mould, McNaughton's first-team appearances were restricted to the early weeks of the season.

Once Hearts had signed Colin McAdam and Billy McKay there was much more competition for places in attack and for the most part McNaughton had to bide his time in the reserves. Towards the end of the season, it was mutually agreed that Brian could leave to become a part-time player again.

Jimmy Sandison

Born, 22/6/65
Signed, 1983
Place of Birth, Edinburgh
Number of Appearances – 2 (3)

The 20-year-old defender first caught the eye when he had an outstanding game at sweeper in the public trial match staged by Hearts before the season began.

The former Edinburgh Emmet player was more often seen at full back and it was in the right-hand role against Celtic and St Mirren in August that he made his first-team appearances in the Premier Division.

The Board and Commercial Staff

Chairman – Wallace Mercer

In May of 1981, when Wallace Mercer invested £400,000 of his own cash in Hearts, it was difficult if not impossible to imagine the turn around that the new majority shareholder would engineer at Tynecastle over the space of the next five years.

Hearts were a forlorn crew, on the brink of a part-time existence, when Mercer took over the wheel of the ship. Yet in the current financial year, Hearts will report a profit on trading for the fourth consecutive season and it will be bigger than last year's. More significantly, Hearts have become a watertight business proposition without having to resort to selling players to balance the books.

Of course the playing success achieved by Hearts in 1985/86 was outwith even Mercer's planning capabilities, but undoubtedly he did create the environment in which a young management team of Alex MacDonald and Sandy Jardine could thrive.

Mercer's straightforward business techniques helped Hearts to reduce their overheads while finding other sources of income. The gamble he took in investing cash in new players from the very beginning paid off because the customers were persuaded to come and watch an improved team.

And come they did in ever-increasing numbers. The hard core of the Hearts' support at each match was raised to over the 15,000 mark only five years after the attendances for an entire season at Tynecastle amounted to 120,000.

Hearts may still be in the red at the bank, but the business itself is worth around £4 million and Hearts don't owe a penny to another club. A family area was built adjacent to the enclosure last year – the club have more than 3,000 junior members – and Mercer has been successful in attracting the right kind of customers.

A football club is sticking its neck out if it talks about having licked the problem of hooliganism, but there's no doubt that the anti-social element in the Hearts support are more of a minority than ever before.

Perhaps even more significant than Mercer's work on the business side were his efforts in restoring a voice to the club. Some would argue that it was a voice too readily heard on too many subjects, but few detractors could take issue with the chairman's ability to generate publicity.

Whether it was raffling houses and cars to drum up attendances in the

Wallace Mercer

early days, or else arguing the case on behalf of the Premier Division's full-time clubs for a breakaway that never happened, Mercer was persistently involved in the promotion of Hearts.

In short, he made sure the club was heard as well as seen. Mercer was courteous and helpful to sportswriters who were staggered to have their calls returned. And he carved out a new image for Hearts which played on the club's great traditions while at the same time stressing a more youthful, dynamic approach.

Mercer, with tongue-in-cheek no doubt, once described Hearts as a workers' co-operative. Profit was linked to performance, he said, and the more the players won the more they earned. In 1985/86, they earned plenty.

As far as the man himself was concerned, Mercer's most endearing quality was a sense of fun. He enjoys the gift of being able to laugh at himself, and as a relative newcomer to the commercial world of sport, was always willing to take on board the advice of those with greater experience.

But Mercer is nothing if not a hard headed business man as well as a punter, and the recent euphoria about Hearts' progress won't be allowed to influence the way he thinks the club should be run.

Last December in America, Mercer laid the plans for Hearts until the summer of 1987. He made it clear that short-term results wouldn't have any bearing on that strategy. But just as he's done through the dark days at Tynecastle as well as the bright, Mercer will continue to put his money where his mouth is for Hearts.

Director – Bobby Parker

The 60-year-old former chairman had particular reason to relish season 1985/86. He was named as the club's first honorary director at the annual general meeting where he was presented with a decanter and glasses for his services to Hearts.

Bobby Parker has been connected with Hearts in one capacity or another for 40 years since his transfer as a player from Partick Thistle in 1946. He captained Hearts' League Cup winning side of 1954 which beat Motherwell 4-2 and after his playing days assisted in the running of the reserves.

An Edinburgh newsagent, he joined the board in the spring of 1970 and was the only director to survive the period of upheaval after Wallace Mercer's takeover. His knowledge of what went on in the dressing-room made him an invaluable voice in the boardroom and for many he was the link between the great Hearts' side of the 1950s and the present team.

Director – Douglas Park

The second largest shareholder at Tynecastle was a well known figure in Scottish football long before he joined the Hearts' board. His company, Parks of Hamilton, was involved in supplying buses for many sets of clubs and supporters and Park was often seen on the SFA's international charter-flights to games abroad.

As a successful businessman in the transport world, Park was able to play an important role in assisting Hearts to increase their support at away matches. His buses helped Hearts to set up a novel system whereby unattached supporters could travel to games outwith Edinburgh at a cheap price. This was a significant development at a time when manager Alex MacDonald referred to the club's increasing support as the team's 12th man.

Director – Pilmar Smith

Recruited to the Tynecastle board after Wallace Mercer's arrival, the long-time Hearts supporter and shareholder brought a vigorous enthusiasm to the boardroom. If Mercer was the main ideas man, Pilmar Smith often helped to put those thoughts into working practice.

An Edinburgh bookmaker who had been on friendly terms with many of the Hearts players around the time Dave Mackay was inspiring the side, Smith was regarded at Tynecastle as the director who liaised between the club and the supporters. He was involved in the fight against hooliganism and helped with the introduction of innovations like video cameras.

Commercial Director – Robin Fry

When Wallace Mercer moved to fill the post of commercial director at Tynecastle in the summer of 1981 he made it quite clear that he regarded the position as being on a par with the manager's job in terms of importance.

Hearts sifted through some 65 applications before deciding that the man they'd brought north from Hereford to become the club's lottery consultant was the ideal candidate.

Fry had a football background with Bristol City and Bristol Rovers and won an England schoolboy cap. But it was in developing the commercial appeal of Hearts that he made his mark, winning important sponsorship deals and helping to supplement the club's income from gate money. He is assisted by the commercial manager, Charles Burnett.

Club Secretary – Les Porteous

The club secretary was formerly an administrative employee of the National Union of Mineworkers. His experience with Newtongrange Star helped him win the post as successor to Bill Devine in 1980. Les Porteous was one of the busiest employees at Tynecastle in the course of a season where the club was frequently involved in all-ticket matches. An able, cheerful individual with a helpful manner, Porteous helped to provide a sound administrative base for Hearts' expanding fortunes.

Europe

Hearts have qualified to play in Europe for the eighth time next season though it has to be said that the club has an undistinguished record against foreign competitors.

It is equally true that the club has not been favoured by good draws. In their last attempt at the European Cup in 1960, their Portuguese opponents were not well known but Benfica had a great side which went on to win the Champions Cup.

Standard Liège, Inter Milan, Saragossa, Hamburg and, more recently, Paris St. Germain were outstanding teams. The current Hearts team learned much from their exploits against the French team, inspired by the brilliance of Yugoslav inside forward Safet Susic.

St. Germain became French champions for the first time in 1986 as a result of a long, unbeaten run.

Hearts have never gone beyond the second round of any tournament, winning six of their 22 ties. Easily the most satisfying was the comeback against Lokomotive Leipzig in 1976 when a 2-0 defeat was transformed into a 5-3 aggregate victory.

EUROPEAN CUP
1958–59
| Standard Liège | (A) 1-5 |
| Standard Liège | (H) 2-1 |

1960–61
| Benfica | (H) 1-2 |
| Benfica | (A) 0-3 |

FAIRS CUP
1961–62
St. Gilloise	(A) 2-0
St. Gilloise	(H) 3-1
Inter Milan	(H) 0-1
Inter Milan	(A) 0-4

1963–64
Lausanne	(A) 2-2
Lausanne	(H) 2-2
*Lausanne	(A) 2-3

Hearts exert pressure against Paris St. Germain at Tynecastle with Jimmy Bone, now at Arbroath, leading the challenge which ended in a 2-2 draw

1965–66

Valerengen	(H)	1-0
Valerengen	(A)	3-1
Saragossa	(H)	3-3
Saragossa	(A)	2-2
★ Saragossa	(A)	0-1

★ Lost toss for ground advantage

CUP WINNERS CUP
1976–77

Lokomotive Leipzig	(A)	0-2
Lokomotive Leipzig	(H)	5-1
Hamburg	(A)	2-4
Hamburg	(H)	1-4

UEFA CUP
1984–85

| Paris St. Germain | (A) 0-4 |
| Paris St. Germain | (H) 2-2 |

	P	W	D	L	F	A
Home	10	4	3	3	20	17
Away	12	2	2	8	14	31
	22	6	5	11	34	48

European action at Tynecastle last season as John Robertson shoots first of his two goals against Paris St. Germain

Early Days

Hearts were founded in the early 1870s. They became full members of the Scottish Football Association five years later and founder members of the Scottish League in 1890. They originally played in red, white and blue but made the switch to maroon when amalgamating with players from the St Andrew club.

The romantic name, Heart of Midlothian, was actually the moniker given to an old jail situated near Edinburgh's St Giles in the 18th century. The site is marked today by a large heart outlined in the stones near the cathedral.

A novel by Sir Walter Scott, *The Heart of Midlothian*, kept the name in the forefront of attention at a time when football clubs knew the value of a grand title. In later years the colloquial form, Hearts, was more widely used.

Even today in Edinburgh this is likely to be pronounced like the name of a car hire firm – ie 'Away the Hertz'. A new generation of Hearts' fans, using rhyming slang, have nicknamed the club 'The Jam Tarts' or 'The Jams'. It is doubtful if this inane tag would have gone down particularly well with Tom Purdie, the team's first captain, who chose the dazzling Heart of Midlothian.

Hearts moved into Tynecastle in 1881 when an advert in *The Scotsman* advised would-be customers that ladies would be admitted free. From the very beginning, it seems, the club were chasing a family audience!

Hearts first won the Scottish Cup in 1891, beating Dumbarton 1-0 in the final with the following team – Fairbairn; Adams, Goodfellow; Begbie, McPherson, Hill; Taylor, Mason, Russell, Scott and Baird.

By 1894-5 Hearts had secured victory in the Scottish League Championship, a feat they were to repeat in 1897 but would not achieve again until the late 1950s.

Undoubtedly the big game of this period was the Scottish Cup final of 1896 when the Heart of Midlothian met their Edinburgh rivals Hibernian. It was played at Logie Green near Powderhall in Edinburgh before more than 16,000 spectators. Hearts won 3-1 with the following side – Fairbairn; McCartney, Mirk; Begbie, Russell, Hogg; McLaren, Baird, Michael, King, Walker.

Hearts had a new star when they chased the championship the following season. Bobby Walker, a right winger from Dalry Primrose, supplied the crosses which helped Hearts to score the goals that gave them a two-point advantage over Hibs at the end of the 18-match schedule.

Walker was still a key figure in 1901 when Hearts beat Celtic 4-3 in the Scottish Cup final. He was regarded as the best player in Europe at the time because of his running, passing and shooting strengths. He won 29 caps for Scotland, which in those days was a considerable tally.

It is an odd coincidence that Hearts traditionally do well in the Scottish Cup when there is a six in the year. As happened this season when Hearts had to change from their normal maroon and white colours in the final against Aberdeen, against Third Lanark in 1906 Hearts wore blue. Backed by a vociferous support from Edinburgh, Hearts won 1-0 against the Glasgow side 80 years ago with this team – Philip; McNaught, Philip; McLaren, Thomson, Dickson; Couper, Walker, Menzies, D. Wilson, G. Wilson.

The Terrible Trio

If Gary Mackay, John Robertson and Craig Levein all came on to the transfer market at once, Hearts would expect to collect around £1 million in transfer fees.

Quite what kind of sum the three most famous players in Hearts' history – the terrible trio of Alfie Conn, Willie Bauld and Jimmy Wardhaugh – would attract had they been around in today's market is hard to assess. Thirty years ago you couldn't have prised them away from Tynecastle for love nor money.

We know that Dave McLean, the Hearts manager of the day, splashed out the regal sum of £200 to sign all three individuals. Willie Bauld began his career with Musselburgh Athletic. Those who saw him in action at that early stage might have been fooled by the deceptively lazy style – but when Bauld headed the ball it was like watching a rocket being launched.

He resisted a move to join Sunderland and completed his apprenticeship with Newtongrange Stars and Edinburgh City. Hearts moved in for Bauld in 1946. Jimmy Wardhaugh signed the same year after being captain of the British A.T.C. at Geneva. Alfie Conn had arrived two years earlier, a Prestonpans lad who had played for Bathgate Academy and was signed from Inveresk Juveniles.

All three players fitted into McLean's plan to change Hearts' fortunes by putting the emphasis on young full-time footballers in peak physical condition. It was clear from the very start that Conn, Bauld and Wardhaugh were something special. The first time they played together Hearts routed East Fife 6-1.

This was at a juncture, similar to the period when Alex MacDonald and Sandy Jardine took over the management of the club in the 1980s, when Hearts' fortunes were at a dismally low ebb. The club hadn't won anything since the Scottish Cup victory of 1906.

It was another managerial partnership that helped to change things in the 1950s. For assisting Dave McLean was one of Hearts' legendary figures. Tommy Walker went on to succeed McLean as manager and with his self-effacing, dignified air was always known to the players as simply Mr Walker.

Of Walker's own playing career, possibly the most famous incident came when as a 19-year-old he turned out for Scotland against England at Wembley. It was 1936 and a penalty was awarded to Scotland. Walker was asked to take it and he placed the ball three times as the wind swirled.

It's the early days of the 'Terrible Trio'. In this team group – Back row: Cox, Parker, Brown, Dougan, Mackenzie, Laing. Front: Sloan, Conn, Bauld, Wardhaugh, Williams

Amidst unbearable tension, the unflappable Walker stroked the ball past the English goalkeeper to give Scotland victory.

Walker was made manager of Hearts in 1951 and the club only had three years to wait for their breakthrough in the League Cup of season 1953-54. Hearts qualified from a section which included Celtic, Falkirk and Dundee. In the quarter-finals they dismissed St Johnstone before beating Airdrie in the semi-final at Easter Road.

The final was at Hampden where the following team beat Motherwell 4-2: Duff; Parker, Mackenzie; Mackay, Glidden and Cumming; Souness, Conn, Bauld, Wardhaugh and Urquhart.

The day was a personal triumph for Bauld who scored three times while Wardhaugh got the fourth. It was an era when Hearts firepower was so considerable that victories in double figures were not unknown.

There were those who wondered if time stopped when Bauld went up to head the ball, so stunning was his ability to hang in the air. The Tynecastle

Tommy Walker –
a Tynecastle
legend

faithful hailed him as King Willie Bauld that night the team brought the
League Cup back to Edinburgh's North British Hotel.

For all the individual brilliance Conn, Bauld and Wardhaugh brought to
Hearts forward play, it was their collective impact that Tommy Walker
remembered best. 'They always appeared to play as one', he recalled.
'Their individual skills, expertise, positional sense and scoring ability were
simply dovetailed into one unit.'

In 1956 it was an Alfie Conn goal that set Hearts on their way to eventual
triumph in the Scottish Cup campaign of that year. Other goals from John
Cumming and Johnny Hamilton dismissed Forfar Athletic. Hearts went on
to take Stirling apart 5-0 in the next round with goals from Bauld, Conn,
Wardhaugh, Cumming and Young.

Not even Rangers could stand in the way of this mighty goalscoring

The triumphant procession with the Scottish Cup won by beating Celtic in 1956

machine as a brace from Bauld and one apiece from Conn and Crawford put Hearts into a semi-final against Raith Rovers at Easter Road.

The first match was drawn 0-0. In the replay two goals from Wardhaugh and a Crawford header near the end secured Hearts' place in the final against Celtic. There were 132,840 spectators at Hampden to watch an epic contest.

It was Ian Crawford who set Hearts on the way to victory with two first-half goals. But Celtic came back into things when Haughney scored and there was alarm in the Hearts' camp when Cumming was badly cut above the brow.

The iron-man, of course, played on clutching a sponge to wipe the blood from his eyes. With just 10 minutes remaining, Hearts made sure of victory with a goal from Conn. The team was – Duff; Kirk, Mackenzie; Mackay, Glidden, Cumming; Young, Conn, Bauld, Wardhaugh, Crawford.

With two Cups under their belts, Hearts set out in season 1957-58 with the aim of adding the League Championship to their credentials.

Three famous Hearts and Scotland players – Willie Bauld, Jim Cruickshank and Jimmy Wardhaugh

Apart from the terrible trio, Hearts were a team of stars. Alex Young, Dave Mackay, Jimmy Murray, John Cumming, Andy Bowman, Johnny Hamilton, Ian Crawford and Bobby Blackwood all had goals to contribute in the course of a season when Hearts struck hard and often.

It was an astonishing year with a goal procession that won't ever be seen again. Among Hearts' livelier displays, were a 9-0 win over East Fife, a 9-1 win against Falkirk, 8-0 against Queen's Park and 7-2 against Third Lanark.

Hearts made a profit that season of £12,925, though the figures that will last through the years are those that contain that record number of 132 championship goals.

In season 1958-59 Hearts won the League Cup again with a team which featured five survivors from the side that made the breakthrough against Motherwell in the same competition four years previously – namely Mackay, Glidden, Cumming, Bauld and Wardhaugh.

This time Hearts beat Partick Thistle 5-1, Bauld scoring twice, Jimmy Murray getting two and Johnny Hamilton the other. However it was John Cumming's performance that caught the eye as Hearts claimed another honour and established their reputation as the best team in Scotland.

Champions – and Record Breakers

Hearts like to become champions with a bit of style and, when they ended a 61-year wait in 1958, the players set a new scoring record and the highest points total for 34 matches.

No other team stood a chance against the free-scoring Hearts who had 132 goals and 62 points to their credit. Only Clyde beat them and the Shawfield side actually won three of the six points dropped in the one-horse race.

Hearts had 15 straight wins during an unbeaten stretch of 22 games which produced the incredible total of 42 points.

Third Lanark, Kilmarnock and Motherwell won a point apiece during the season but it was goals all the way for the Gorgie boys. They scored 43 more than Rangers who were 13 points behind.

Jimmy Wardhaugh had three of the six hat-tricks and netted 28 goals, one more than Jimmy Murray who had one hat trick along with Dave Mackay and Alex Young. Murray (27) and Young (24) contributed a total of 79 goals with the twinkle-toed Wardhaugh.

On nine occasions, the Tynecastle team scored five goals or more to outclass the opposition.

Hearts used 22 players and only Young played in every match though Murray missed one in a glorious season which earned him a place in Scotland's World Cup team for Sweden.

1957–58

	P	W	D	L	F	A	Pts
HEARTS	34	29	4	1	132	29	62
Rangers	34	22	5	7	89	49	49
Celtic	34	19	8	7	84	47	46
Clyde	34	18	6	10	84	61	42
Kilmarnock	34	14	9	11	60	55	37
Partick Thistle	34	17	3	14	69	71	37
Raith Rovers	34	14	7	13	66	56	35
Motherwell	34	12	8	14	68	67	32
Hibernian	34	13	5	16	59	60	31
Falkirk	34	11	9	14	64	82	31
Dundee	34	13	5	16	49	65	31
Aberdeen	34	14	2	18	68	76	30
St. Mirren	34	11	8	15	59	66	30
Third Lanark	34	13	4	17	69	88	30
Queen of the South	34	12	5	17	61	72	29
Airdrie	34	13	2	19	71	92	28
East Fife	34	10	3	21	45	88	23
Queens Park	34	4	1	29	41	114	9

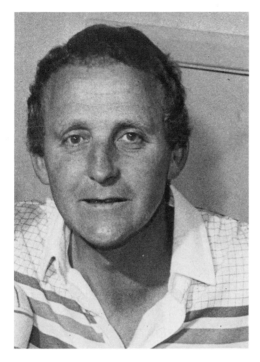

Alex Young... the Golden Boy who won further fame with Everton. Now a successful businessman in Edinburgh

Hearts were winning 10-club championships in the last century though teams met only twice in those days.

Their first championship was won in 1895, assisted by a run of 11 matches without defeat which was more than half the programme.

Willie Michael scored 10 of their 50 goals and Hearts had five points to spare over Celtic. There were three Edinburgh clubs in the competition, the others being St. Bernards and Leith Athletic.

1894–95

	P	W	D	L	F	A	Pts
HEARTS	18	15	1	2	50	18	31
Celtic	18	11	4	3	50	29	26
Rangers	18	10	2	6	41	26	22
Third Lanark	18	10	1	7	51	39	21
St. Mirren	18	9	1	8	34	34	19
St. Bernards	18	8	1	9	37	40	17
Clyde	18	8	0	10	38	47	16
Dundee	18	6	2	10	28	33	14
Leith Athletic	18	3	1	14	32	64	7
Dumbarton	18	3	1	14	27	58	7

Two seasons later, Hearts were champions for the second time though it was a tight finish with their greatest city rivals.

Hibernian would have taken the title if they had won one of their last fixtures at Tynecastle but Hearts resisted their challenge and scored the only goal.

Only those two points separated the sides at the final count.

1896–97

	P	W	D	L	F	A	Pts
HEARTS	18	13	2	3	47	22	28
Hibernian	18	12	2	4	50	20	26
Rangers	18	11	3	4	64	30	25
Celtic	18	10	4	4	42	18	24
Dundee	18	10	2	6	38	30	22
St. Mirren	18	9	1	8	30	29	19
St. Bernards	18	7	0	11	32	40	14
Third Lanark	18	5	1	12	29	46	11
Clyde	18	4	0	14	27	65	8
Aberdeen	18	1	1	16	21	88	3

It was generally accepted that when Hearts last won the championship in 1960 they were not quite the same force as the 1958 winners. For all that Hearts were rarely out of the headlines in the course of a notable season that began with the spectacular coup of Gordon Smith's transfer from Hibs.

When Smith made his debut for Hearts' reserves that August there were no fewer than 12,000 people at Tynecastle and the winger had to be smuggled out of the ground to avoid a huge posse of autograph hunters. If Smith's most famous days were at Easter Road, he was to recall in later life that the football he enjoyed playing most was at Tynecastle — mainly because less was expected of him.

Smith's arrival inevitably meant there were goings as well as comings at Tynecastle. Jimmy Wardhaugh asked for a transfer and got one to Dunfermline. Bobby Rankin moved to Third Lanark and younger players like Billy Higgins were given their chance.

What the 1960 championship winning side had in common with the present team above all else was a long unbeaten run. In all matches including friendlies that autumn Hearts embarked on an unbeaten run of 26 games that finally came to an end when St Mirren won at Tynecastle in December.

However Hearts gained a measure of revenge at Love Street in the spring when they clinched the title in Paisley. It took a Willie Bauld goal in the very last minute of a dramatic game which finished 4–4 to bring the championship flag back to Edinburgh again.

The team that day was – Marshall; Kirk, Thomson; Cumming, Milne, Higgins; Smith, Young, Bauld, McFadzean, Crawford.

In total Hearts used only 16 players that season in the league; the others involved were Bowman, Murray, Brown, Blackwood and Hamilton.

Manager Tommy Walker, who had guided Hearts to their sixth major honour since 1954, put the success of the 1960 campaign down to 'a full season of consistency'.

Bobby Parker, who is now a member of the board at Tynecastle, was a reserve team coach with Hearts 26 years ago and his greatest memory of the difference between then and now was the number of goals scored.

When Bauld produced that equaliser against St Mirren, it was Hearts' 100th goal in a 32-game season. Even at that they weren't to top scorers. Hibs claimed the honour, but their leaky defence ensured the Easter Road team finished no higher than seventh.

1959–60

	P	W	D	L	F	A	Pts
HEARTS	34	23	8	3	102	51	54
Kilmarnock	34	24	2	8	67	45	50
Rangers	34	17	8	9	72	38	42
Dundee	34	16	10	8	70	49	42
Motherwell	34	16	8	10	71	61	40
Clyde	34	15	9	10	77	69	39
Hibernian	34	14	7	13	106	75	35
Ayr United	34	14	6	14	65	73	34
Celtic	34	12	9	13	73	59	33
Partick Thistle	34	14	4	16	54	78	32
Raith Rovers	34	14	3	17	64	62	31
Third Lanark	34	13	4	17	75	83	30
Dunfermline	34	10	9	15	72	80	29
St. Mirren	34	11	6	17	78	86	28
Aberdeen	34	11	6	17	54	72	28
Airdrie	34	11	6	17	56	80	28
Stirling Albion	34	7	8	19	55	72	22
Arbroath	34	4	7	23	38	106	15

League Cup joy in 1962 as Willie Hamilton and Norrie Davidson show off the silverware in the company of John Harvey, Gordon Marshall, Willie Polland, John Cumming, Danny Paton, Willie Wallace, Davie Holt and Johnny Hamilton

Hearts had to wait until October of 1962 to add their seventh trophy in Walker's reign as manager. It came in the League Cup final against Kilmarnock at Hampden when they won the competition for the fourth time in nine years.

Kilmarnock's hopes were diminished even before a ball was kicked when Sneddon, their influential playmaker, was declared unfit. He gave Kilmarnock their shape, much in the same way Willie Hamilton did for Hearts.

Years later in a hotel foyer in Poland, Jock Stein, who was manager of Scotland at the time, waxed lyrical about Hamilton's many talents. 'Willie Hamilton was the greatest', said Stein, 'because he could tackle, dribble, pass and shoot. The Baxters, and the Johnstones each had the one thing they could do brilliantly. But Hamilton had it all.'

Certainly against Kilmarnock, it was the mercurial Hamilton who inspired Hearts to victory. It was from his run in the 25th minute, jinking past Richmond and McGrory, that Norrie Davidson got on the end of a

144

header for the final's only goal.

Today the match is probably remembered best for the goal that never was, 'scored' by Beattie in the last minute. Kilmarnock felt it was a clean header, but referee Tommy Wharton spotted a handling offence and the Cup went back to Tynecastle.

The consensus was that Hearts had deserved to win but had lived dangerously late on in the match by trying to defend their narrow lead rather than attacking with their usual freedom of expression. The Hearts team was – Marshall; Polland, Holt; Cumming, Barry, Higgins; Wallace, Paton, Davidson, W. Hamilton, J. Hamilton.

Tommy Walker commented afterwards that the players 'realised what was needed to operate as a unit. They put on a new veneer and appreciated the importance of team work.'

It was a tribute that would prove to be just as valid a comment 24 years later on regarding the individuals blended into a team by Alex MacDonald and Sandy Jardine with such remarkable precision.

The Award Winners

Apart from Hearts' achievements as a team, the 1985–86 season was particularly noticeable for the number of individual awards won by the management team and staff at Tynecastle. In fact throughout the year Hearts picked up more gongs than a Hollywood blockbuster on Oscar night.

The most prestigious award of the football season is the Scottish Football Writers' Association player of the year. On the night of the game's major social occasion at a dinner in Glasgow's Albany Hotel, Sandy Jardine became the first ever Hearts player to receive this trophy.

If it was a new experience for the club — and with typical modesty Jardine made it clear that he felt the honour belonged to Hearts as much as himself — it was in fact the third time that Hearts' assistant player-manager had been connected with the prize.

In 1974 he was a member of the Scotland World Cup squad that won the trophy jointly before leaving for West Germany. And a year later as a Rangers player he won the accolade outright. By the age of 37 and with more than 1000 games of senior football under his belt, it would have been understandable if Jardine's thoughts had been turning to retirement presentations rather than player of the year awards.

But Jardine had always made it clear than no one would know better than himself when the time had come to go. And in 1986 his distinguished service to Hearts made him only the second player in the 21-year existence of the football writers' award to become a winner twice. (The other individual was John Greig of Rangers.)

The biggest prize open to a manager in football north of the border is the manager of the year presentation in the Scottish Brewers Football Personality awards.

At a lunch in Glasgow in the week before the Scottish Cup final, Alex MacDonald made another breakthrough for the Edinburgh club when he became the first Hearts manager ever to earn the sobriquet of manager of the year.

Throughout his career, first as a splendidly inventive midfield player and then as a retiring player-coach who blossomed into an outstanding manager, there had been a tendency to underestimate MacDonald's abilities. It was a situation that needed rectifying, and in 1986 MacDonald's shrewd work with Hearts received deserved public acclaim.

The end of season prizes, of course, were preceded by others secured by members of the Hearts' staff. During the winter at the Skol Sportsman and Sportswoman dinner in Glasgow's Holiday Inn, Sandy Jardine was again the recipient of a special award for his services to football. On a star-studded occasion, Jardine's popularity was in no doubt throughout the sporting world when he received the biggest ovation of the night from an audience of fellow athletes, journalists and sponsors.

Jardine was also the Scottish Brewers player of the month for January; it was a notable start to 1986 for the Hearts management team as the New Year also heralded Alex MacDonald's second manager of the month award. He had earlier taken the prize in November for steering Hearts through an unbeaten run.

Of course MacDonald and Jardine were not the only individuals at Tynecastle to get a pat on the back. In December Craig Levein was the personality player of the month for a series of consistently outstanding displays in defence.

While the young centre-back was one of the main reasons why Hearts lost so few goals in the course of the season, John Colquhoun was one of the team's prize opportunists in front of the goal. He was named the personality player of the month for February — the third consecutive month that a Hearts player had been so honoured.

Fine Fare, the sponsors of the Scottish League, also ran a season-long series of awards for the young footballer of the month. Here again Hearts were fêted more often than any other Scottish club during 1985–86. In November Craig Levein won for his stylish defensive work. In January an in-form Gary Mackay won for the marvellous performances he'd delivered against Dundee United and Aberdeen. And in March John Robertson's relentless sequence of goals took the prize to Tynecastle yet again.

All told Hearts won eight monthly awards as well as the end-of-term annual prizes. And possibly the most significant recognition of all came when Alex Ferguson picked Craig Levein, Gary Mackay and John Robertson for Scottish international squads. Levein was a member of the party that travelled to play Israel in Tel Aviv while Robertson and Mackay were both on the bench against Holland in Eindhoven.

Hearts 1985/86 Roll Call of Honour

Scottish Football Writers' Association Player of the Year —Sandy Jardine.

Scottish Brewers Football Personality Manager of the Year — Alex MacDonald.

Scottish Brewers Monthly Personality Awards (Manager) —
November — Alex MacDonald
January — Alex MacDonald.

Scottish Brewers Monthly Personality Awards (Player) —
December — Craig Levein
January — Sandy Jardine
February — John Colquhoun.

Fine Fare Young Footballer of the Month Awards —
November — Craig Levein
January — Gary Mackay
March — John Robertson.

Young Player of the Year — Craig Levein
Voted by his fellow professionals.

Complete League Record

	P	W	L	D	Goals F	A	Pts	Position
1890–1	18	6	10	2	31	37	14	6
1891–2	22	15	3	4	64	36	34	3
1892–3	18	8	8	2	39	42	18	4
1893–4	18	11	3	4	46	32	26	2
1894–5	18	15	2	1	50	18	31	1
1895–6	18	11	7	0	68	35	22	4
1896–7	18	13	3	2	47	22	28	1
1897–8	18	8	6	4	54	33	20	4
1898–9	18	12	4	2	56	30	26	2
1899–1900	18	10	5	3	41	24	23	4
1900–1	20	5	11	4	22	30	14	10
1901–2	18	10	6	2	32	21	22	3
1902–3	22	11	5	6	46	27	28	4
1903–4	26	18	5	3	63	35	39	2
1904–5	26	11	12	3	46	44	25	7
1905–6	30	18	5	7	64	27	43	2
1906–7	34	11	10	13	46	43	35	9
1907–8	34	11	17	6	50	22	28	11
1908–9	34	12	14	8	54	49	32	11
1909–10	34	12	15	7	59	50	31	11
1910–11	34	8	8	8	42	59	24	14
1911–12	34	16	10	8	54	40	40	4
1912–13	34	17	10	7	71	43	41	3
1913–14	38	23	7	8	70	29	54	3
1914–15	38	27	4	7	83	32	61	2

Glorious Hearts

	P	W	L	D	Goals F	A	Pts	Position
1915–16	37	20	11	6	66	45	46	5
1916–17	38	14	20	4	44	59	32	14
1917–18	34	14	16	4	41	58	32	10
1918–19	34	14	11	9	59	52	37	7
1919–20	42	14	19	9	57	72	37	15
1920–1	42	20	12	10	74	49	50	3
1921–2	42	11	21	10	50	60	32	19
1922–3	38	11	12	15	51	50	37	11
1923–4	38	14	14	10	61	50	38	9
1924–5	38	12	15	11	65	69	35	10
1925–6	38	21	9	8	87	56	50	3
1926–7	38	12	15	11	65	64	35	13
1927–8	38	20	11	7	89	50	47	4
1928–9	38	19	10	9	91	57	47	4
1929–30	38	14	15	9	69	69	37	10
1930–1	38	19	13	6	90	63	44	5
1931–2	38	17	16	5	63	61	39	8
1932–3	38	21	9	8	84	51	50	3
1933–4	38	17	11	10	86	59	44	6
1934–5	38	20	8	10	87	52	50	3
1935–6	38	20	11	7	88	55	47	5
1936–7	38	24	11	3	99	60	51	5
1937–8	38	26	6	6	90	50	58	2
1938–9	38	20	13	5	98	70	45	4
1939–40	29	18	7	4	104	66	40	2
1940–1	30	12	13	5	64	71	29	10
1941–2	30	14	12	4	85	72	32	5
1942–3	30	12	11	7	68	64	31	7

					Goals			
	P	W	L	D	F	A	Pts	Position
1943–4	30	14	9	7	67	50	35	4
1944–5	30	14	9	7	75	60	35	5
1945–6	30	11	11	8	63	57	30	7
1946–7	30	16	8	6	52	43	38	4
1947–8	30	10	12	8	37	42	28	9
1948–9	30	12	12	6	64	54	30	8
1949–50	30	20	7	3	86	40	43	3
1950–1	30	16	9	5	72	45	37	4
1951–2	30	14	9	7	69	53	35	4
1952–3	30	12	12	6	59	50	30	4
1953–4	30	16	8	6	70	45	38	2
1954–5	30	16	7	7	74	45	39	4
1955–6	34	19	8	7	99	47	45	3
1956–7	34	24	5	5	81	48	53	2
1957–8	34	29	1	4	132	29	62	1
1958–9	34	21	7	6	92	51	48	2
1959–60	34	23	3	8	102	51	54	1
1960–1	34	13	13	8	51	53	34	8
1961–2	34	16	12	6	54	49	38	6
1962–3	34	17	8	2	85	59	43	5
1963–4	34	19	6	9	74	40	47	4
1964–5	34	22	6	6	90	49	50	2
1965–6	34	13	9	12	56	48	38	7
1966–7	34	11	15	8	39	48	30	11
1967–8	34	13	17	4	56	61	30	12
1968–9	34	14	12	8	52	64	36	8
1969–70	34	13	9	12	50	36	38	4
1970–1	34	13	14	7	41	40	33	11

	P	W	L	D	Goals F	A	Pts	Position
1971–2	34	13	8	13	53	49	39	6
1972–3	34	12	16	6	39	50	30	10
1973–4	34	14	10	10	54	43	38	6
1974–5	34	11	10	13	47	52	35	8
1975–6	36	13	14	9	39	45	39	5
1976–7	36	7	16	13	49	66	27	9
1977–8	39	24	5	10	77	42	58	2
1978–9	36	8	21	7	39	71	23	9
1979–80	39	20	6	13	58	39	53	1
1980–1	36	6	24	6	27	71	18	10
1981–2	39	21	10	8	65	37	50	3
1982–3	39	22	7	10	79	38	54	2
1983–4	36	10	10	16	38	47	36	5
1984–5	36	13	18	5	47	64	31	7
1985–6	36	20	6	10	59	33	50	2

Complete Scottish Cup Record

1875–6
(After two draws with 3rd E.R.V., both went into second round)

Hearts 0	Drumpellier 2

1876–7
Did not play

1877–8

Hearts 1	Hibernians 2

1878–9

Hearts 3	Swifts 1
Hearts 1	Thistle 0
Hearts 2	Arbroath 1

Scratched

1879–80
Walk-over (3rd E.R.V. scratched)

Hearts 3	Brunswick 2
Hearts 1	Hibernians 2

1880–1

Hearts 3	Brunswick 1
Bye	
Hearts 5	Hibernians 3
Hearts 3	Cambuslang 0
Hearts 0	Arthurlie 4

1881–2

Hearts 1	St. Bernards 2

1882–3

Hearts 4	St. Bernards 3
Hearts 14	Addiewell 0
Hearts 1	Vale of Leven 8

1883–4

Hearts 8	Brunswick 0
Hearts 4	Newcastleton 1
Hearts 1	Hibernians 4

1884–5
Bye
Expelled after Dunfermline protest

1885–6

Hearts 1	St. Bernards 0
(after protested game)	
Hearts 1	Hibernians 2

1886–7

Hearts 7	Edina 1
Hearts 2	Broxburn Thistle 1
Hearts 1	Hibernians 5

1887–8

Hearts 4	Norton Park 1
Bye	
Hearts 1	Hibernians 1
Hearts 3	Hibernians 1
Hearts 1	St. Mirren 1
Hearts 2	St. Mirren 2
Hearts 2	St. Mirren 2
Hearts 2	St. Mirren 4

1888-9

Hearts 1	Bo'ness 0
Hearts 7	Erin Rovers 0
Hearts 2	Broxburn 2
Hearts 2	Broxburn 0
Hearts 1	Campsie 3

1889-90

Hearts 3	St. Bernards 0
Hearts 4	Bellstane Birds 1
Hearts 5	Champfleurie 0
Hearts 9	Alloa Athletic 1
Hearts 1	Vale of Leven 3

1890-1

	Hearts 7	Raith Rovers 2
Walk-over; Burntisland Thistle scratched		
	Hearts 3	Methlan Park 0
	Hearts 4	Ayr 3
	Hearts 5	Morton 1
	Hearts 3	East Stirlingshire 1
SF	Hearts 4	Third Lanark 1
Final	Hearts 1	Dumbarton 0

1891-2

Hearts 8	Clyde 0
(after a protested game Hearts won 3-1)	
Hearts 5	Broxburn Shamrock 4
Hearts 4	Renton 4
Hearts 2	Renton 2
Hearts 2	Renton 3

1892-3

Hearts 1	Stenhousemuir 1
Hearts 8	Stenhousemuir 0
Hearts 4	Motherwell 2
Hearts 1	Queen's Park 1
Hearts 2	Queen's Park 5

1893–4

	Hearts 0	St. Mirren 1

1894–5

	Hearts 2	Rangers 1
	Hearts 6	Abercorn 1
	Hearts 4	King's Park 2
SF	Hearts 0	St. Bernards 0
	Hearts 0	St. Bernards 1

1895–6

	Hearts 12	Blantyre 1
	Hearts 5	Ayr 1
	Hearts 4	Arbroath 0
SF	Hearts 1	St. Bernards 0
Final	Hearts 3	Hibernians 1

1896–7

	Hearts 2	Clyde 0
	Hearts 2	Third Lanark 5

1897–8

	Hearts 8	Lochee United 0
	Hearts 4	Morton 1
	Hearts 0	Dundee 3

1898–9

	Hearts 1	Rangers 4

1899–1900

	Hearts 0	St. Mirren 0
	Hearts 3	St. Mirren 0
	Hearts 1	Hibernians 1
	Hearts 2	Hibernians 1
	Hearts 2	Third Lanark 1
SF	Hearts 1	Queen's Park 2

1900–1

	Hearts 7		Mossend Swifts 0
	Hearts 2		Queen's Park 1
	Hearts 5		Port Glasgow Athletic 1
SF	Hearts 1		Hibernians 1
	Hearts 2		Hibernians 1
Final	Hearts 4		Celtic 3

1901–2

	Hearts 0		Cowdenbeath 0
	Hearts 3		Cowdenbeath 0
	Hearts 4		Third Lanark 1
	Hearts 1		Celtic 1
	Hearts 1		Celtic 2

1902–3

	Hearts 2		Clyde 1
	Hearts 4		Ayr 2
	Hearts 2		Third Lanark 1
SF	Hearts 0		Dundee 0
	Hearts 1		Dundee 0
Final	Hearts 1		Rangers 1
	Hearts 0		Rangers 0
	Hearts 0		Rangers 2

1903–4

	Hearts 2		Rangers 3

1904–5

	Hearts 3		Dundee 1
	Hearts 1		St. Mirren 2

1905–6

	Hearts 4		Nithsdale Wanderers 1
	Hearts 3		Beith 0
	Hearts 2		Celtic 1
SF	Hearts 2		Port Glasgow Athletic 0
Final	Hearts 1		Third Lanark 0

1906–7

	Hearts 0	Airdrieonians 0
	Hearts 2	Airdrieonians 0
	Hearts 0	Kilmarnock 0
	Hearts 2	Kilmarnock 1
	Hearts 2	Raith Rovers 2
	Hearts 1	Raith Rovers 0
SF	Hearts 1	Queen's Park 0
Final	Hearts 0	Celtic 3

1907–8

Hearts 4   St. Johnstone 1
Hearts 4   Port Glasgow Athletic 0
Hearts 1   St. Mirren 3
(after game abandoned — St. Mirren led 1-0)

1908–9

Hearts 2   Kilmarnock 1
Hearts 0   Aidrieonians 2

1908–9

Hearts 2   Kilmarnock 1
Hearts 0   Airdrieonians 2

1909–10

Hearts 4   Bathgate 0
Hearts 2   St. Mirren 2
Hearts 0   St. Mirren 0
Hearts 4   St. Mirren 0
Hearts 0   Hibernians 1
(after game abandoned — Hearts led 1-0)

1910–11

Hearts 1   Clyde 1
Hearts 0   Clyde 1

1911–12

	Hearts 0	Hibernians 0
	Hearts 1	Hibernians 1
	(abandoned in falling snow)	
	Hearts 1	Hibernians 1
	Hearts 3	Hibernians 1
	Hearts 1	Dundee 0
	Hearts 1	Morton 0
SF	Hearts 0	Celtic 3

1912–13
Bye

	Hearts 3	Dunfermline Athletic 1
	Hearts 2	Kilmarnock 0
	Hearts 1	Celtic 0
SF	Hearts 0	Falkirk 1

1913–14
Bye

	Hearts 0	Raith Rovers 2

1919–20

Hearts 5	Nithsdale Wanderers 1
Hearts 2	Falkirk 0
Hearts 0	Aberdeen 1

1920–1
Bye

	Hearts 1	Clyde 1
	Hearts 0	Clyde 0
	Hearts 3	Clyde 2
	Hearts 1	Hamilton Academicals 0
	Hearts 2	Celtic 1
SF	Hearts 0	Partick Thistle 0
	Hearts 0	Partick Thistle 0
	Hearts 0	Partick Thistle 2

1921–2

Hearts 2	Arthurlie 1
Hearts 2	Broxburn 2
Hearts 2	Broxburn 2
Hearts 3	Broxburn 1
Hearts 0	Rangers 4

1922–3

Hearts 6	Thornhill 0
Hearts 2	Bo'ness 3

1923–4

Hearts 0	Third Lanark 0
Hearts 3	Third Lanark 0
Hearts 6	Galston 0
Hearts 3	Clyde 1
Hearts 1	Falkirk 2

1924–5

Hearts 4	Leith Athletic 1
Hearts 1	Kilmarnock 2

1925–6

Hearts 1	Dundee United 1
Hearts 6	Dundee United 0
Hearts 5	Alloa Athletic 2
Hearts 0	Celtic 4

1926–7

Hearts 2	Clyde 3

1927–8

Hearts 2	St. Johnstone 2
Hearts 1	St. Johnstone 0
Hearts 7	Forres Mechanics 0
Hearts 1	Motherwell 2

1928-9

	Hearts 0	Airdrieonians 2

1929-30

	Hearts 1	Clydebank 0
	Hearts 0	St. Bernards 0
	Hearts 5	St. Bernards 0
	Hearts 3	Hibernians 1
	Hearts 2	Dundee 2
	Hearts 4	Dundee 0
SF	Hearts 1	Rangers 4

1930-1

Hearts 9	Stenhousemuir 1
Hearts 2	Kilmarnock 3

1931-2

Hearts 13	Lochgelly 3
Hearts 4	Cowdenbeath 1
Hearts 0	Rangers 1

1932-3

Hearts 3	Solway Star 0
Hearts 6	Airdrieonians 0
Hearts 2	St. Johnstone 0
Hearts 0	Hibernians 0
Hearts 2	Hibernians 0
Hearts 0	Celtic 0
Hearts 1	Celtic 2

1933-4

Hearts 5	Montrose 1
Hearts 2	Queens's Park 1
Hearts 0	Rangers 0
Hearts 1	Rangers 2

Glorious Hearts

1934-5

	Hearts 7	Solway Star 0
	Hearts 2	Kilmarnock 0
	Hearts 2	Dundee United 2
	Hearts 4	Dundee United 2
	Hearts 3	Airdrieonians 2
SF	Hearts 1	Rangers 1
	Hearts 0	Rangers 2

1935-6

Hearts 0   Third Lanark 2

1936-7

Hearts 3   St. Bernards 1
Hearts 15   King's Park 0
Hearts 1   Hamilton Academicals 2

1937-8

Hearts 1   Dundee United 3

1938-9

Hearts 14   Penicuik Athletic 2
Hearts 14   Elgin City 1
Hearts 2   Celtic 2
Hearts 1   Celtic 2

1939-40

Hearts 2   St. Johnstone 2
Hearts 4   St. Johnstone 2
Hearts 2   Raith Rovers 1
Hearts 0   Airdrieonians 0
Hearts 2   Airdrieonians 2
Hearts 3   Airdrieonians 4

1946-7

Hearts 3   St. Johnstone 0
Bye
Hearts 2   Cowdenbeath 0
Hearts 1   Arbroath 2

1947–8
Hearts 4	Dundee 2
Hearts 1	Airdrieonians 2

1948–9
Hearts 4	Airdrieonians 1
Hearts 3	Third Lanark 1
Hearts 3	Dumbarton 0
Hearts 2	Dundee 4

1949–50
Hearts 1	Dundee 1
Hearts 2	Dundee 1
Hearts 1	Aberdeen 3

1950–1
Hearts 3	Alloa Athletic 2
Hearts 5	East Stirlingshire 1
Hearts 1	Celtic 2

1951–2
Bye
	Hearts 1	Raith Rovers 0
	Hearts 3	Queen of the South 1
	Hearts 2	Airdrieonians 2
	Hearts 6	Airdrieonians 4
SF	Hearts 1	Motherwell 1
	Hearts 1	Motherwell 1
	Hearts 1	Motherwell 3

1952–3
Bye
	Hearts 1	Raith Rovers 0
	Hearts 2	Montrose 1
	Hearts 2	Queen of the South 1
SF	Hearts 1	Rangers 2

1953–4
Bye

Hearts 3	Fraserburgh 0
Hearts 2	Queen of the South 1
Hearts 0	Aberdeen 4

1954–5

Hearts 5	Hibernian 0
Hearts 6	Buckie Thistle 0
Hearts 1	Aberdeen 1
Hearts 1	Aberdeen 2

1955–6

	Hearts 3	Forfar Athletic 0
	Hearts 5	Stirling Albion 0
	Hearts 4	Rangers 0
SF	Raith Rovers 0	Hearts 0
	Raith Rovers 0	Hearts 3
Final	Hearts 3	Celtic 1

1956–7

Hearts 0	Rangers 4

1957–8

Hearts 2	East Fife 1
Hearts 4	Albion Rovers 1
Hearts 3	Hibernians 4

1958–9

Queen of the South 1	Hearts 3
Rangers 3	Hearts 2

1959–60

Hearts 1	Kilmarnock 1
Kilmarnock 2	Hearts 1

1960–1

Hearts 9	Tarff Rovers 0
Kilmarnock 1	Hearts 2
Partick Thistle 1	Hearts 2
Hearts 0	St. Mirren 1

1961–2

Vale of Leven 0	Hearts 5
Hearts 3	Celtic 4

1962–3

Forfar Athletic 1	Hearts 3
Celtic 3	Hearts 1

1963–4

Queen of the South 0	Hearts 3
Motherwell 3	Hearts 3
Hearts 1	Motherwell 2

1964–5

Falkirk 0	Hearts 3
Morton 3	Hearts 3
Hearts 2	Morton 0
Motherwell 1	Hearts 0

1965–6

Hearts 2	Clyde 1
Hearts 2	Hibernian 1
Hearts 3	Celtic 3
Celtic 3	Hearts 1

1966–7

Hearts 0	Dundee United 3

1967–8

	Hearts 4	Brechin City 1
	Dundee United 5	Hearts 6
	Rangers 1	Hearts 1
	Hearts 1	Rangers 0
SF	Hearts 1	Morton 1
	Hearts 2	Morton 1
Final	Dunfermline 3	Hearts 1

1968–9

Dundee 1	Hearts 2
Rangers 2	Hearts 0

1969–70

Montrose 1	Hearts 1
Hearts 1	Montrose 0
Kilmarnock 2	Hearts 0

1970–1

Hearts 3	Stranraer 0
Hearts 1	Hibernian 2

1971–2

Hearts 2	St. Johnstone 0
Hearts 4	Clydebank 0
Celtic 1	Hearts 1
Hearts 0	Celtic 1

1972–3

Hearts 0	Airdrie 0
Airdrie 3	Hearts 1

1973–4

Hearts 3	Clyde 1
Hearts 1	Partick Thistle 1
Partick Thistle 1	Hearts 4
Hearts 1	Ayr United 1
Ayr United 1	Hearts 2

SF	Hearts 1	Dundee United 1
	Hearts 2	Dundee United 4

1974–5

	Hearts 2	Kilmarnock 0
	Queen of the South 0	Hearts 2
	Hearts 1	Dundee 1
	Dundee 3	Hearts 2

1975–6

	Hearts 2	Clyde 2
	Clyde 0	Hearts 1
	Hearts 3	Stirling Albion 0
	Montrose 2	Hearts 2
	Hearts 2	Montrose 2
	Montrose 1	Hearts 2
SF	Hearts 0	Dumbarton 0
	Hearts 3	Dumbarton 0
Final	Hearts 1	Rangers 3

1976–7

	Hearts 1	Dumbarton 1
	Dumbarton 0	Hearts 1
	Hearts 1	Clydebank 0
	Hearts 0	East Fife 0
	East Fife 2	Hearts 3
SF	Hearts 0	Rangers 2

1977–8

	Airdrie 2	Hearts 3
	Dumbarton 1	Hearts 1
	Hearts 0	Dumbarton 1

1978–9

	Raith Rovers 0	Hearts 2
	Hearts 1	Morton 1
	Morton 0	Hearts 1
	Hibernians 2	Hearts 1

1979–80

Alloa 0	Hearts 1
Hearts 2	Stirling Albion 0
Rangers 6	Hearts 1

1980–1

Morton 0	Hearts 0
Hearts 1	Morton 3

1981–2

East Stirling 1	Hearts 4
Hearts 0	Forfar Athletic 1

1982–3

Queen of the South 1	Hearts 1
Hearts 1	Queen of the South 0
Hearts 2	East Fife 1
Celtic 4	Hearts 1

1983–4

Hearts 2	Partick Thistle 0
Dundee United 2	Hearts 1

1984–5

Hearts 6	Inverness Caley 0
Brechin City 1	Hearts 1
Hearts 1	Brechin City 0
Hearts 1	Aberdeen 1
Aberdeen 1	Hearts 0

1985–6

	Hearts 3	Rangers 2
	Hamilton 1	Hearts 2
	Hearts 4	St. Mirren 1
SF	Hearts 1	Dundee United 0
Final	Hearts 0	Aberdeen 3

Season Analysis

PREMIER LEAGUE

Date	Fixture		Result	Attendance
Aug 10	Celtic	H	1-1	21,786
Aug 17	St. Mirren	A	2-6	6,273
Aug 24	Rangers	A	1-3	35,483
Aug 31	Hibernian	H	2-1	17,457
Sep 7	Aberdeen	A	0-3	11,890
Sep 14	Dundee United	H	2-0	7,617
Sep 21	Motherwell	A	1-2	4,806
Sep 28	Clydebank	A	0-1	3,641
Oct 5	Dundee	H	1-1	8,512
Oct 12	Celtic	A	1-0	26,683
Oct 19	St. Mirren	H	3-0	8,638
Oct 30	Aberdeen	H	1-0	12,886
Nov 2	Dundee United	A	1-1	10,142
Nov 9	Hibernian	A	0-0	19,776
Nov 16	Rangers	H	3-0	23,083
Nov 23	Motherwell	H	3-0	10,119
Nov 30	Clydebank	H	4-1	10,267
Dec 7	Dundee	A	1-1	10,780
Dec 14	Celtic	H	1-1	22,163
Dec 21	St. Mirren	H	1-0	6,498
Dec 28	Rangers	A	2-0	33,410
Jan 1	Hibernian	H	3-1	25,605
Jan 4	Motherwell	A	3-1	9,850
Jan 11	Dundee United	H	1-1	19,043
Jan 18	Aberdeen	A	1-0	21,460
Feb 1	Clydebank	A	1-1	6,095
Feb 8	Dundee	H	3-1	15,365
Feb 22	Celtic	A	1-1	45,346
Mar 15	Motherwell	H	2-0	12,071
Mar 22	Hibernian	A	2-1	21,100
Mar 25	St. Mirren	H	3-0	13,287
Mar 29	Rangers	H	3-1	24,735
Apr 12	Dundee United	A	3-0	20,515
Apr 20	Aberdeen	H	1-1	19,047
Apr 26	Clydebank	H	1-0	20,198
May 3	Dundee	A	0-2	19,567

169

SKOL LEAGUE CUP

Aug 20	Montrose	A	3-1	1,992
Aug 27	Stirling Albion	H	2-1	4,479
			(extra-time)	
Sep 4	Aberdeen	A	0-1	13,066

SCOTTISH CUP

Jan 25	Rangers	H	3-2	27,442
Mar 3	Hamilton	A	2-1	10,000
Mar 9	St. Mirren	H	4-1	20,655
Apr 5	Dundee United	N	1-0	30,872
May 10	Aberdeen	N	0-3	62,841

APPEARANCES

	League		Scottish Cup		League Cup	
	App	*Goals*	*App*	*Goals*	*App*	*Goals*
Smith	36	—	5	—	3	—
Colquhoun	36	8	5	2	2(1)	1
S. Jardine	35	—	5	—	3	—
Robertson	34(1)	20	5	4	3	1
Levein	33	2	5	—	3	—
Clark	33	12	5	—	2	—
G. Mackay	30(2)	4	5	2	2	—
Berry	32	2	5	—	—	—
Kidd	28	—	5	—	2	1
Black	23(6)	2	5	1	2	—
Whittaker	24	1	4	—	3	—
I. Jardine	19(4)	7	1(1)	—	—	—
Watson	8(4)	—	—(1)	—	3	—
R. McDonald	10	2	—(1)	—	3	—
Cowie	8	—	—	—	1	—
Cherry	3(2)	—	—	—	—(2)	1
McAdam	—(5)	—	—(1)	1	—	—
Sandison	2(1)	—	—	—	—(2)	—
McNaughton	2(2)	—	—	1	1	—
W. McKay	—(3)	—	—(1)	—	—	—
A. MacDonald	—(1)	—	—	—	—	—